yes, it's a scrapbook!

CREATIVE ALBUMS, PHOTO DECOR & DECORATIVE JOURNALS

BY DONNA DOWNEY

yes, it's a scrapbook!

by Donna Downey

CK MEDIA

Founding Editor | Stacy Julian
Editor in Chief | Jennafer Martin
Editors | Valerie Pingree, Elisha Snow
Editorial Assistant | Carolyn Jolley
Copy Editor | Mark Zoellner
Art Director | Don Lambson, Cathy Zielske
Graphic Designer | Celeste Rockwood-Jones
Photography | John Luke
Chief Executive Officer | David O'Neil
SVP, Group Publishing Director | Scott Wagner

For information on carrying *Simple Scrapbooks* products in your retail
store, please call (800) 815-3583. For information on ordering *Simple
Scrapbooks* magazine, call toll-free (866) 334-8149. *Simple Scrapbooks*
is located at 14850 Pony Express Road, Bluffdale, Utah, 84065. Phone:
(801) 984-2070. Home page: *www.simplescrapbooksmag.com*

Library of Congress Control Number: 2008934191
ISBN-13: 978-1-60140-859-4
ISBN-10: 1-60140-859-5

LEISURE ARTS

Managing Editor | Susan White Sullivan
Special Projects Director | Susan Frantz Wiles
Director of Designer Relations | Debra Nettles
Senior Prepress Director | Mark Hawkins
Publishing Systems Administrator | Becky Riddle
Publishing Systems Assistants | Clint Hanson, John Rose, Keiji
Yumoto, and Carrie East

Vice President and Chief Operating Officer | Tom Siebenmorgen
Director of Corporate Planning and Development | Laticia Mull Dittrich
Vice President, Sales and Marketing | Pam Stebbins
Director of Sales and Services | Margaret Reinold
Vice President, Operations | Jim Dittrich
Comptroller, Operations | Rob Thieme
Retail Customer Service Manager | Stan Raynor
Print Production Manager | Fred F. Pruss

Published by Leisure Arts, Inc., 5701 Ranch Drive, Little Rock,
Arkansas 72223-9633. Phone: (501) 868-8800. Home page:
www.leisurearts.com

editor's note

MY HOME HAS ALWAYS BEEN a place where creativity is deeply nourished. My children know that art is what you make it and there's no right or wrong way to create a work of art. "Perfect just the way I create" is a motto I live by, and each of the projects in this book is a reflection of this motto and a result of my nontraditional approach to scrapbooking.

I'm inspired by all products—not just traditional scrapbooking supplies (although I use those in abundance as well!). I'm always looking for ways to turn ordinary items into scrapbooks, and I get a thrill from simply walking the aisles of my local hardware store and dreaming of what I can do with a wooden rail or a paint can. I tend to see beauty and potential in cast-off treasures from consignment stores, yard sales, and online auctions. What's old is new again!

I hope that as you flip through this book, you'll mark dozens of ideas for creating unique albums, journals, and home décor, as well as inspiration for topics. Don't be afraid to modify any project to fit your needs. Be flexible, have fun, go wild! Then encourage anybody who visits your home to pick up, flip through, and play with each finished project. These aren't museum pieces; they should be dog-eared, threadbare, banged up, and well-worn after six months. If they're not, you should be inviting more people over to visit.

Remember that scrapbooking is less about committing yourself to a hobby and more about sharing the stories of your everyday life in any creative medium. The true nature of scrapbooking is to preserve and display our photo memories. Your life and your loved ones are unique; let your home and your scrapbooks be just as one-of-a-kind.

a guide to the projects

PHOTO DECOR

creative albums

2003 year in review

ALTERED CD ALBUM

This album was the original inspiration for the *Yes, It's a Scrapbook!* series, and proves that when it comes to compiling, arranging, and displaying bound memories, it's good to think outside the box. It's a great way to use those old CDs you don't listen to anymore—and unless someone peels back the paper, no one ever has to know you were once the world's biggest Kenny Loggins fan.

THE DOWNEY FAMILY

2003   2003   2003   2003   2003

a year in review

SUPPLIES

- eight compact discs
- eight 6" x 6" pieces of coordinated patterned paper
- eight 6" x 6" pieces of cardstock
- seven 4" x 6" photos
- stamp pad
- seven metal-rimmed tags with jump rings and 2½" binder ring
- rub-on letters
- stickers, cut to small round tag size

TOOLS

- large circle template
- swivel knife and mat
- hand drill with largest and smallest drill bits
- labeler
- scissors

ADHESIVE

- Xyron machine

MATERIALS

patterned paper (Chatterbox) • metal-rimmed tags (Avery Dennison) • rub-ons (Chartpak) • stickers (Creative Imaginations, Li'l Davis Designs, EK Success) • word plaque (Li'l Davis Designs) • metal letters, word, bookplate (Making Memories) • stamp pad (Ranger Industries) • Coluzzle nested circle template, swivel knife, mat (Provo Craft) • labeler (Dymo) • hand drill (Fiskars)

altered cd album step-by-step

STEP ONE
Use circle template or trace CD to cut eight circles, one from each piece of patterned paper.

STEP TWO
Ink edges of patterned paper (see "Inking" on p. 219) and adhere pieces to one side of each CD. *Note: Use a full-surface adhesive to prevent the edges of your papers and photos from lifting.*

STEP THREE
Use template or CD to round off each photo. *Note: The straight edge of the photo should fit about halfway to three quarters across the CD.* Adhere photos to CD, over patterned paper.

STEP FOUR
Use labeler to create word strips. Adhere word strips along straight edge of photos.

STEP FIVE
Print or write text on cardstock pieces and trim to circles using template or CD. Ink edges and adhere to back of CDs. *Note: If you choose to print your text, create a text box no larger than 3" x 4" (see "Printing Journaling" on p. 220).*

STEP SIX
Using largest drill bit, drill hole at top of each CD for binder ring (see "Craft Hand Drill" on p. 215).

STEP SEVEN
Drill second hole using smallest drill bit. *Note: For a random effect, drill the small hole in a different spot on each CD so that the tags will extend from all sides of your final album.* Thread jump rings with tags through small holes in CDs.

STEP EIGHT
Embellish CDs using rub-ons; embellish small tags using stickers.

STEP NINE
Attach all CDs to large binder ring.

Helpful Tip

When using the Coluzzle template, the large circle template—the 6th circle from the center—is the exact size for the CDs. If you do not have the large template, you can trace a CD and cut by hand or use a smaller circle for your pages.

best friends forever

I've known my best friend Karen for almost 20 years, and that's a lot of late-night chats and secrets.
A friendship like ours deserves a special album, so I created this one, complete with little tags describing
our years together (and the trouble we caused). All you need is one piece of 12" x 12" cardstock to create
the accordion, and, of course, a dear friend to share it.

SUPPLIES

- 12" x 12" piece of cardstock
- two 3" x 6" pieces of chipboard
- two 5" x 8" pieces of patterned paper
- six 3" x 6" pieces of patterned paper
- bookplate and metal frame

- four tags and four eyelets
- four 6" lengths of ribbon
- 18" length of ribbon
- three pre-printed quotes
- one brad and one photo turn

TOOLS

- paper trimmer with scoring blade
- bone folder
- eyelet-setting tools
- large square punch
- sanding block

ADHESIVE

- Xyron machine
- photo tabs
- dots

MATERIALS

patterned paper, pre-printed quotes (KI Memories) • tags (DMD, Inc.) • frame, photo turn (7gypsies) • bookplate (Li'l Davis Designs) • eyelets, brad (Making Memories) • ribbons (May Arts, Textured Trios, The Weathered Door)

Well-behaved women rarely make history.

If you obey all the rules you miss all the fun.
—Katherine Hepburn

Laughter is the shortest distance between two people.
—Victor Borge

I am what I am.
Rosario Morales

accordion pocket album step-by-step

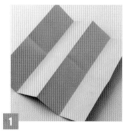

STEP ONE
Fold cardstock in half, using bone folder (see "Bone Folder" on p. 215). Unfold. Accordion-fold lengthwise every 3". Refold cardstock in half.

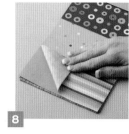

STEP TWO
To create front and back covers, adhere 5" x 8" patterned paper pieces to chipboard, using Xyron machine (see "Wrapping Chipboard Covers" on p. 218). Sand edges.

STEP THREE
Before assembling album, make sure the long, folded edge of accordion-folded cardstock is at the bottom. Attach cover to front flap, making sure it opens to the left.

STEP FOUR
Before adhering back cover, adhere ribbon to back of album. Wrap around album and tie in front.

STEP FIVE
Turn album over and attach back cover over ribbon, securing ribbon in place. *Note: Make sure the cover opens to the right.*

STEP SIX
Using photo tabs, adhere four pieces of 3" x 6" patterned paper to four inside panels.

STEP SEVEN
Adhere two remaining 3" x 6" patterned paper pieces to the back of first and last panels.

STEP EIGHT
Fold top outside corners of first and last panels toward inside creases, and secure using eyelets (see "Setting Eyelets" on p. 219).

STEP NINE
Use square punch to create windows in second and third panels.

STEP TEN
Embellish four tags, using ribbon, photos, patterned paper, and quotes.

STEP ELEVEN
Unfold cardstock. Place tags within open folds of four panels; refold cardstock in half.

STEP TWELVE
Embellish album using additional quotes. Adhere frame with dots. Attach photo turn with brad. Place quotes behind frame and photo turn.

STEP THIRTEEN
Print album title. Mount title and bookplate on cover.

my little book of four-letter words

TAG ALBUM

This little tag book is filled with some of my favorite *clean* four-letter words. It's a scrapbook just for me, and it sits in plain view on my desk. It's the first thing people reach for when they walk into my workspace, and the last thing they put down before they leave. Sure, it's starting to show some signs of wear, but that's the best compliment of all.

SUPPLIES

- 3½" x 6½" tag album
- large letter stickers
- assorted colored cardstock
- coordinated eyelets
  (three per page, two for cover)
- assorted ribbon (6" per tag)
- rub-on letters
- printed twill ribbon
- buckle fastener
- black pen and colored chalk

TOOLS

- paper trimmer
- eyelet-setting tools

ADHESIVE

- photo tabs

MATERIALS

tag book, printed twill ribbon, buckle fastener (7gypsies) • ribbon (Offray, Textured Trios) • rub-ons (Chartpak) • letter stickers (Sticker Studio) • eyelets (Making Memories) • pen (Sakura)

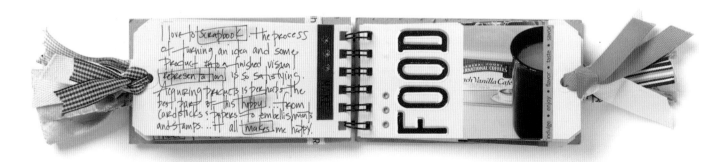

tag album step-by-step

STEP ONE
Trim photos to fit one tag, approximately 2¼" x 3⅛". Adhere photos to the right of each page.

STEP TWO
Use letter stickers to create four-letter words. Place vertically to the left of each photo.

STEP THREE
Print or handwrite two cardstock word strips for each page. Cut and adhere strip next to photo. Cut and adhere strip on back next to spiral binding.

STEP FOUR
Set eyelets through word strip on back, making sure the finished side of the eyelet shows on the front of the tag.

STEP FIVE
Handwrite journaling on the back of each tag. Use chalk to highlight important words.

STEP SIX
Tie ribbon through hole of each tag.

STEP SEVEN
Embellish cover using letter stickers, rub-ons, printed twill ribbon, eyelets, and buckle fastener.

Helpful Tip

Make your own tag book, or buy a pre-made one from companies such as 7gypsies, K&Company, or Rusty Pickle.

coley

Our Grandma Cookie works at the deli counter at the local supermarket and is all the talk every time she pulls one of these grandchildren-filled mini albums from her purse. These scrapbooks fit in the palm of her hand, so she can whip one out sometime between dispensing the Gouda and smoked turkey, to show off these sweet faces. It's the perfect brag book.

SUPPLIES

- four 3½" x 10½" pieces of cardstock
- two 3½" x 3½" slide mounts
- 12" length of ribbon
- rub-on letters and phrases
- definition stickers
- 8" length of ribbon
- metal charm or tag
- stencil letter

TOOLS

- paper trimmer with scoring blade (see "Paper trimmer" on p. 216)
- bone folder

ADHESIVE

- double-sided tape

MATERIALS

slide mounts (Design Originals) • rub-ons, definition stickers, stencil letter (Making Memories) • ribbon (May Arts, Textured Trios)

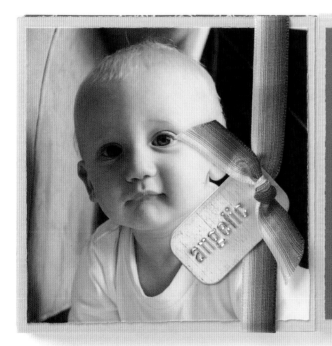

Whether it's Cole. Coley, Coler, Cola, Cole-Baby or Little Man you come smiling and crawling no matter what. Perhaps the happiest and sweetest little boy I have ever seen, it is hard not to squeeze and kiss you every moment of the day. Your expressions are priceless and those meaty little thighs just delicious to nibble on. As you continue to grow and change, it is great to see you develop such a playful personality.

journaled 9.04

slide mount accordion album **step-by-step**

STEP ONE

Score each cardstock strip every 3½". Accordion-fold.

STEP TWO

Adhere accordion strips together by overlapping ends (see "Assembling Accordion Pages" on p. 218).

STEP THREE

Trim any extra panels so that the two ends face up.

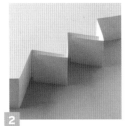

STEP FOUR

Slip photos into slide mounts, and adhere so that the photo is facing out the window.

STEP FIVE

Adhere slide mount to the front of your accordion strip.

STEP SIX

Before adhering back cover, adhere ribbon to back of accordion strip—then wrap around album. Tie in front. Adhere back slide mount to accordion strip, securing ribbon in place.

STEP SEVEN

Trim photos and any journaling to 3¼" squares. Adhere and embellish with rub-ons, ribbon, charm, stencil letter, and stickers.

art

BOUND PAINT CHIP ALBUM

Seems like someone in my house is always painting, drawing, scribbling, or crafting something. The place buzzes with artistic energy, and I always feel compelled to capture it on film. With stacks of multicolor photos to show for my neurosis, I have a creative solution for the photo overload—use ordinary paint chips from your local hardware store to create a scrapbook.

SUPPLIES

- two 5" x 10" pieces of chipboard
- two 7" x 12" pieces of patterned paper
- two 4¾" x 9¾" pieces of cardstock
- two 3" x 10" pieces of cardstock
- 12 3" x 8½" paint chips in assorted colors
- assorted ribbon
- miscellaneous embellishments

TOOLS

- bone folder
- labeler

ADHESIVE

- Xyron machine
- photo tabs
- adhesive remover

MATERIALS

patterned paper (Paper House Productions) • paint chips (Glidden) • ribbon (Paper House Productions, Textured Trios, May Arts) • chipboard, puzzle, wooden letters (Li'l Davis Designs) • rubber stamps (All Night Media, Inkadinkado) • rub-ons (Creative Imaginations) • woven label (me & my BIG ideas) • spiral clip, brad (Making Memories) • word charm (*stampersanonymous.com*) • tile letter (Junkitz) • labeler (Dymo) • adhesive remover (Un-du)

bound paint chip album step-by-step

STEP ONE
Wrap chipboard pieces, using 7" x 12" pieces of patterned paper (see "Wrapping Chipboard Covers" on p. 218).

STEP TWO
Adhere 4¾" x 9¾" pieces of cardstock to inside of each cover to conceal unfinished sides.

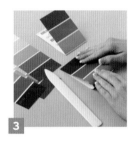

STEP THREE
To create the pages, fold each paint chip in half lengthwise with a bone folder (see "Bone folder" on p. 215).

STEP FOUR
Starting from the bottom, layer six of the paint chips on 3" x 10" piece of cardstock. *Note: The cardstock is a template and will ensure the album is bound correctly.* Arrange chips about 1¼" apart, folded edge flush with the template edge. Leave ¼" space at the top and bottom of the template. Adhere with photo tabs. Layer and adhere six more paint strips on the second template.

STEP FIVE
Take covers and paint strips (on templates) to local office supply or copy store to have the album professionally wire-bound. *Note: Bind the album where the paint chip ends extend past the template. Do not bind on the folds.* Once bound, remove templates from paint chip pages, using adhesive remover.

STEP SIX
Trim photos to 2½" x 3½". Adhere to paint strips. Embellish using ribbon, stickers, charms, and journaling.

STEP SEVEN
Tie ribbons to spine.

understanding 3

CARDBOARD ALBUM

One man's trash is certainly a scrapper's treasure. Pull that cardboard box from your recycling bin, 'cause it's a scrapbook. Layered with texture and sentiment, this album is the perfect complement to my daughter McKenna's rough-and-tumble tomboy exterior and her tender, sensitive spirit. Plus, the texture of the cardboard is just plain cool.

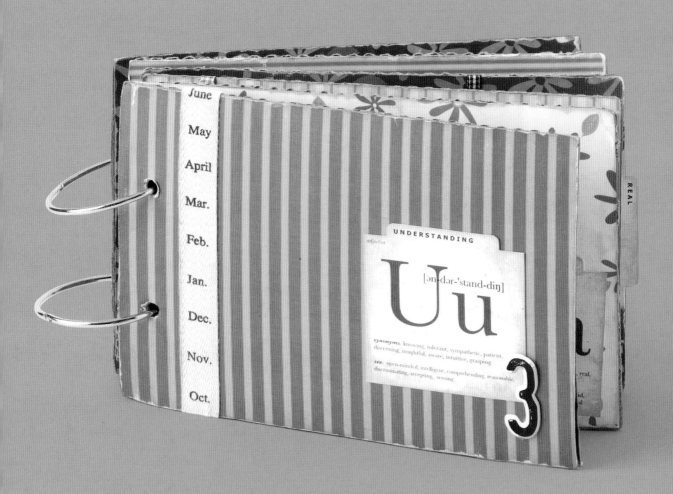

SUPPLIES

- six 6" x 9" pieces of cardboard
- five 5" x 7" pieces of cardboard
- six 6" x 9" pieces of patterned paper
- six 2½" x 4¾" manila tags
- five 5" x 7" pieces of cardstock
- 11 synonym tabs
- 12" length of printed twill ribbon
- two 2½" binder rings
- stamp pad
- number stickers
- assorted ribbon

TOOLS

- hand-held hole punch
- paper trimmer

ADHESIVE

- Xyron machine
- photo tabs

MATERIALS

printed twill, ribbon (7gypsies) • synonym tabs, rub-on date (Autumn Leaves) • number sticker (Sticker Studio) • ribbon (Offray) • Times New Roman font • stamp pad (Ranger Industries)

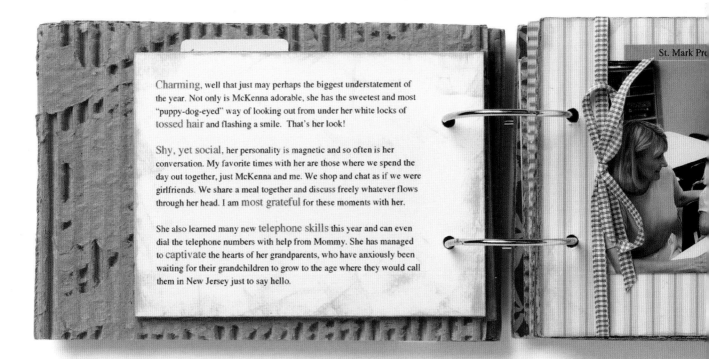

Charming, well that just may perhaps the biggest understatement of the year. Not only is McKenna adorable, she has the sweetest and most "puppy-dog-eyed" way of looking out from under her white locks of tossed hair and flashing a smile. That's her look!

Shy, yet social, her personality is magnetic and so often is her conversation. My favorite times with her are those where we spend the day out together, just McKenna and me. We shop and chat as if we were girlfriends. We share a meal together and discuss freely whatever flows through her head. I am most grateful for these moments with her.

She also learned many new telephone skills this year and can even dial the telephone numbers with help from Mommy. She has managed to captivate the hearts of her grandparents, who have anxiously been waiting for their grandchildren to grow to the age where they would call them in New Jersey just to say hello.

St. Mark Pre

cardboard album step-by-step

STEP ONE

Peel away the top layer of the large and small cardboard pages to reveal the corrugation.

STEP TWO

Adhere 6" x 9" pieces of patterned paper to the smooth (uncorrugated) sides of the larger cardboard pages.

STEP THREE

For the smaller pages, print or write journaling on cardstock and adhere to the smooth sides. Ink edges (see "Inking" on p. 219).

STEP FOUR

Print or write journaling on tags and adhere to the corrugated backs of the larger pages (see "Printing Text on Tags" on p. 220).

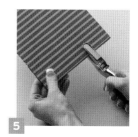

STEP FIVE

For each large page, punch two holes approx. ¾" from the left side of the page, and 1¾" from the top and bottom. For each small page, punch two holes approx. ¾" from the left side of the page, and 1½" from the top and bottom. *Note: Make sure that the journaling is on the back of all the pages.*

STEP SIX

Place pages on binder rings, alternating large and small pages.

STEP SEVEN

Add photos and inked synonym tabs to the front of each page. Tie ribbons around a few pages.

STEP EIGHT

Embellish cover using twill ribbon, inked synonym tab, and number sticker.

St. Mark Preschool   teachers: Mrs. Haake & Mrs. Buck

he biggest understatement of
she has the sweetest and most
m under her white locks of
her look!

netic and so often is her
are those where we spend the
We shop and chat as if we were
discuss freely whatever flows
r these moments with her.

kills this year and can even
Mommy. She has managed
ts, who have anxiously been
the age where they would call

FRIEND

['frend] **Ff**

synonyms: buddy, partner, intimate, confidant, familiar,
acquaintance, mate, cater-cousin, side kick

see: amigo, best friend, alter-ego, ally, colleague

REAL

simply payton

CD TIN ALBUM

Dangling from a hook next to my daughter's bed, this album has affectionately become known as Payton's "shiny round me book." Every night it's her book of choice before bed, and even though at three she can't read a word of it, she flips through it again and again, asking me to read it to her. For Payton, it's the best bedtime story in the world.

SUPPLIES

- round CD tin
- two 12" x 12" pieces of white cardstock
- 12" x 12" piece of patterned paper
- 6" x 6" piece of pre-printed transparency
- 24" length of ribbon
- metal-rimmed vellum tag
- jump ring
- two ³⁄₁₆" eyelets
- reinforcement labels

TOOLS

- large circle template
- swivel knife and mat
- hand drill and largest drill bit
- compact disc (optional)
- eyelet-setting tools
- paper trimmer
- 3" circle punch

ADHESIVE

- photo tabs

MATERIALS

CD tin (Scrapbooks 'N More) • patterned paper, pre-printed transparency (Creative Imaginations) • ribbon (Offray) • metal-rimmed tag, eyelets, jump ring (Making Memories) • Univers Light Ultra Condensed font • Coluzzle nested circle template, swivel knife, mat (Provo Craft) • hand drill (Fiskars)

cd tin album step-by-step

STEP ONE
Cut each sheet of 12" x 12" cardstock into four 6" squares. Create appropriate-sized text boxes. Print or write text and journaling on both sides of squares (see "Printing Journaling" on p. 220). Use circle template (see "Cutting template" on p. 215) or trace CD to cut four circles from each sheet. *Note: You will have a total of eight circles.*

STEP TWO
Cut circle from printed transparency.

STEP THREE
Drill holes through the closed CD tin. *Note: You'll need to secure the tin with a clamp, or have someone hold the tin in place while you drill.*

STEP FOUR
Set an eyelet in both the top and bottom of the tin, making sure to set the finished side of the eyelet on the outside of the tin.

STEP FIVE
Use the tin lid to mark where to drill holes on circle pages, including the transparency. Mark first page and drill through all nine pages at once.

STEP SIX
Adhere reinforcement labels around the drilled holes on both the front and back of each page.

STEP SEVEN
Trace and cut four circles from patterned paper. Cut circles in half and adhere half circle to one-half of each page.

STEP EIGHT
Punch a photo for each page, using jumbo circle punch. Adhere photo to page.

STEP NINE
Print or write title on the vellum tag (see "Printing Text on Tags" on p. 220). Add jump ring.

STEP TEN
Thread ribbon through tin, pages, transparency and jump ring. Tie in bow.

Helpful Tip
The Coluzzle nested circle template has eight circles to choose from. The sixth circle from the center happens to be the exact size of a CD. If you don't have this template-based cutting system, you can always trace a CD and cut by hand.

grandma stephan

CIGAR BOX ALBUM

I had covered a cigar box with decorative paper and it sat on my desk for about a month. I would walk past it and say, "That really looks pretty," and keep on walking. About this time I was interviewing my husband's grandmother about her life, knowing that her story would make a great keepsake one day. I typed it all up on my computer and tucked it away in a cyber file. Finally one day, it made sense: the two things, the cigar box and the interview, just had to go together.

SUPPLIES

- 9½" x 7" cigar box
- three 12" x 12" pieces of patterned paper
- five 6" x 8½" pieces of chipboard
- 11 8½" x 11" pieces of cardstock
- two 2" elastic cords with metal stops
- drawer pull
- stamp pad

TOOLS

- foam brush
- paper towels
- brayer
- hand drill with large and second smallest drill bits
- labeler
- screwdriver
- sanding block
- craft knife

ADHESIVE

- decoupage adhesive
- Xyron machine
- photo tabs

MATERIALS

patterned paper (Daisy D's Paper Company, K&Company) • elastics, index tabs (7gypsies) • hand drill (Fiskars) • labeler (Dymo) • GF Halda Normal font • decoupage adhesive (Plaid)

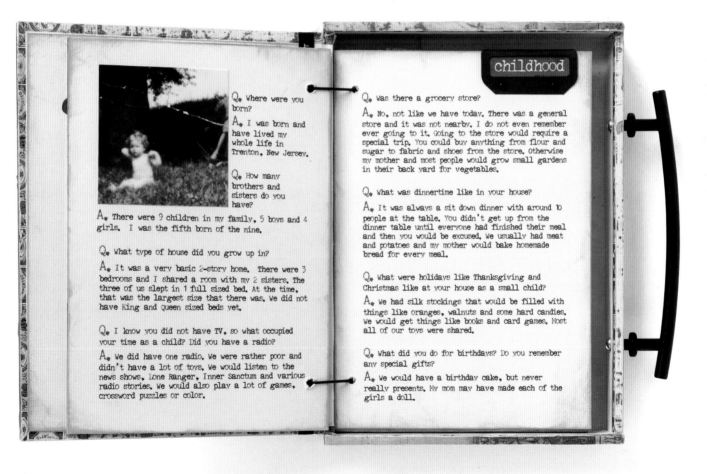

childhood

Q. Where were you born?

A. I was born and have lived my whole life in Trenton, New Jersey.

Q. How many brothers and sisters do you have?

A. There were 9 children in my family, 5 boys and 4 girls. I was the fifth born of the nine.

Q. What type of house did you grow up in?

A. It was a very basic 2-story home. There were 3 bedrooms and I shared a room with my 2 sisters. The three of us slept in 1 full sized bed. At the time, that was the largest size that there was. We did not have King and Queen sized beds yet.

Q. I know you did not have TV, so what occupied your time as a child? Did you have a radio?

A. We did have one radio. We were rather poor and didn't have a lot of toys. We would listen to the news shows, Lone Ranger, Inner Sanctum and various radio stories. We would also play a lot of games, crossword puzzles or color.

Q. Was there a grocery store?

A. No, not like we have today. There was a general store and it was not nearby. I do not even remember ever going to it. Going to the store would require a special trip. You could buy anything from flour and sugar to fabric and shoes from the store. Otherwise my mother and most people would grow small gardens in their back yard for vegetables.

Q. What was dinnertime like in your house?

A. It was always a sit down dinner with around 10 people at the table. You didn't get up from the dinner table until everyone had finished their meal and then you would be excused. We usually had meat and potatoes and my mother would bake homemade bread for every meal.

Q. What were holidays like Thanksgiving and Christmas like at your house as a small child?

A. We had silk stockings that would be filled with things like oranges, walnuts and some hard candies. We would get things like books and card games. Most all of our toys were shared.

Q. What did you do for birthdays? Do you remember any special gifts?

A. We would have a birthday cake, but never really presents. My mom may have made each of the girls a doll.

cigar box album step-by-step

STEP ONE

Trim patterned paper to fit each of the four small sides and the back of the box. *Note: You may want to cut your paper slightly larger than your surface areas, then use a sanding block to sand away the over-hanging edges. This will also create a nice aged look.* Brush a moderate coat of decoupage adhesive on box sides and adhere paper. Firmly press in place and smooth with paper towel, making sure to wipe away any excess adhesive. Use brayer to roll over surface and smooth away any trapped air bubbles.

STEP TWO

Trim patterned paper to fit the top of the box. Adhere using decoupage adhesive. Use a craft knife to cut the paper so the lid can open.

STEP THREE

Let dry in the open position. Gently sand the edges to remove any excess glue.

STEP FOUR

Drill two holes in the box front with a large bit, and install drawer pull. *Note: Drawer pulls usually come with coordinating screws. Depending on the thickness of your box, you may need to purchase shorter-length screws.*

STEP FIVE

With smaller drill bit, drill two holes each through box lid and base (approx. $\frac{3}{4}$" from the spine and $1\frac{3}{8}$" from each side).

STEP SIX

Print album title on cardstock. Trim cardstock $\frac{1}{4}$" smaller than inside box lid on all sides. Ink edges and adhere to inside lid. Use labeler to create strip of text. Place along bottom edge of cardstock where lid meets base.

STEP SEVEN

To create album pages, print text on cardstock, leaving room for photos. Trim cardstock to 6" x 8½". Ink edges and adhere photos.

STEP EIGHT

Adhere cardstock pages, one each to the front and back of chipboard pieces.

STEP NINE

Using small bit, drill holes through pages approx. ½" from side and 1" from top and bottom (see photo). Thread elastic through the bottom of the box, up through the pages, and through the top of the box.

Helpful Tip

If you don't have a cigar box, you can use a stationery or gift box.

a room with a view

PLEXIGLAS ALBUM

I remember seeing a really cool restaurant menu made from Plexiglas. That's why I found myself in a hardware store asking, "Excuse me, sir, do you cut Plexiglas sheets?" Sure enough, 10 minutes later I had a stack of Plexiglas and the beginnings of a new album that shows off my scrapbooking room.

SUPPLIES

- one roll, clear 4" packing tape
- 16" x 24" piece of Plexiglas cut into six 6" x 8" pieces
- six photocopied photographs
- six 6" x 8" pieces of white cardstock
- six 24" lengths of assorted ribbon
- 2" binder ring

TOOLS

- hand drill and large drill bit
- paper trimmer
- water bucket and paper towels
- bone folder

ADHESIVE

- glue stick
- photo tabs

MATERIALS

packing tape (3M) • hand drill (Fiskars) • ribbon (Offray, Textured Trios, May Arts) • Arial font

product

Without a doubt, I am first and foremost inspired by product, and I simply love having them displayed to look at on my shelves. Most times I will create an entire album, or concept an idea before ever knowing what will fill its pages. I feel the most creative freedom when allowing myself to scrapbook this way. I get great satisfaction from finding a new product and creating an entire project around it.

circle letters

quare letters

the best things come in small packages

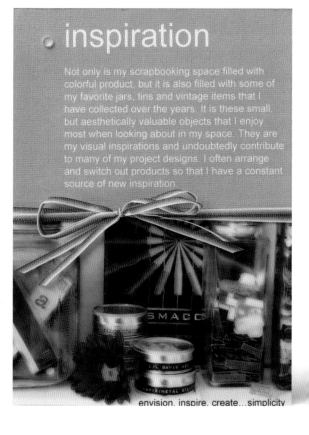

inspiration

Not only is my scrapbooking space filled with colorful product, but it is also filled with some of my favorite jars, tins and vintage items that I have collected over the years. It is these small, but aesthetically valuable objects that I enjoy most when looking about in my space. They are my visual inspirations and undoubtedly contribute to many of my project designs. I often arrange and switch out products so that I have a constant source of new inspiration.

envision, inspire, create...simplicity

plexiglas album step-by-step

STEP ONE
To transfer image, cut and apply clear packing tape over a photocopied image. *Note: Image MUST be photocopied. Pictures printed from a laser or ink-jet printer will not transfer.* Use a bone folder or straight edge ruler to ensure that there are no bubbles in your tape.

STEP TWO
Soak paper with tape in a bucket of warm water for at least 10 min. While the paper is submerged in water, rub your fingers vigorously along the back of tape to remove the paper. *Note: Remove all paper or the tape will not stick.* Repeat for each photo.

STEP THREE
Gently shake off excess water from tape and set on a paper towel, sticky side up. Let dry. *Note: Once tape is dry, it will regain its stickiness.*

STEP FOUR
Firmly press tape to Plexiglas page. *Note: Darker portions of image will tend to be less sticky, due to the amount of toner that was transferred.* Use glue stick to apply adhesive to the less-sticky portions of your tape.

STEP FIVE
Print title and journaling on the top half of cardstock (see "Printing Reverse Text" on p. 220).

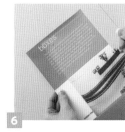

STEP SIX
Place (do not adhere) printed cardstock behind the Plexiglas.

STEP SEVEN
Drill a hole through the upper left corner of the Plexiglas and cardstock. *Note: Use a clamp to secure the Plexiglas as you drill, or have someone hold it for you.*

STEP EIGHT
Secure cardstock to the back of the Plexiglas with ribbon. Tie in front. Adhere ribbon to Plexiglas with photo tabs. Place completed pages on a large binder ring.

Helpful Tip
I used 4" packing tape on this project. If you don't have that size, use two strips of 2" packing tape, placed side by side.

signs of home

SPIRAL-BOUND ALBUM

Going back to my childhood home always triggers a whirlwind of emotions. Everything appears smaller than I remember, and I'm immediately transported back in time to the pizza joint where I wiped mozzarella off my chin or the 7-Eleven where I guzzled a lot of Big Gulps. But the first thing I always look for are the signs—specifically the green and white signs along the New Jersey Parkway—that indicate I'm almost home. This is the kind of scrapbook that unleashes a flood of memories.

SUPPLIES

- two 7" x 12" pieces of patterned paper
- two 5" x 10" pieces of chipboard
- two 4¾" x 9¾" pieces of cardstock
- 8½" x 11" pieces of cardstock in two coordinated shades
- small metal frame

TOOLS

- paper trimmer

ADHESIVE

- Xyron machine
- photo tabs

MATERIALS

patterned paper (Chatterbox) • metal frame (Making Memories)

DON'S PIZZA KING

DON'S PIZZA KING IS AN ICON. A SMALL PIZZA PARLOR THAT OFFERED VIDEO GAMES, A JUKEBOX AND SHELTER FROM THE COLD. MANY A SODA AND SLICES WERE HAD HANGING OUT WITH FRIENDS...ON ST. PATRICK'S DAY THEY WOULD SERVE GREEN PIZZA.

COMO LAKE

ON SUNDAYS AFTER CHURCH, WITH A BAG OF STALE BREAD IN HAND, MOM AND I WOULD HEAD TO COMO LAKE TO FEED THE DUCKS AND GEESE.

spiral-bound album step-by-step

STEP ONE
To create the front and back covers, use patterned paper to cover chipboard (see "Wrapping Chipboard Covers" on p. 218).

STEP TWO
Adhere cardstock to unfinished sides of covers.

STEP THREE
Print text on 8½" x 11" cardstock, then trim each page to 5" x 10".

STEP FOUR
Cut 10" x ⅛" strips of cardstock and adhere between the title and journaling on each page.

STEP FIVE
Trim photos to 4" squares. Mat with cardstock, leaving ¼" border. Adhere to page. *Note: Keep the page design the same throughout the album. Alternate two coordinating shades of cardstock for a simple, balanced look.*

STEP SIX
Embellish the cover with metal frame and title.

STEP SEVEN
Sandwich the pages between the front and back covers, and have the album professionally wire-bound at a local office supply or copy store. *Note: Call ahead to make sure they can bind books.*

Helpful Tip
To type journaling for each page, change page orientation to landscape. Create a 5" square text box and place it on the far left of the page. Type your text, so that it's right justified. And be sure to leave a space for the cardstock strip between the page title and the journaling.

before i was a mom

GATED ALBUM

Although it's hard for my kids to believe, I had a life before I became a mom. Just to prove the point (and to revel in a little nostalgia), I customized a pre-made album by trimming its full-sized page in half and added plenty of photos and journaling about those days before sticky high-chairs, boo-boos, and exhaustion.

SUPPLIES

- gated album
- cardstock
- coordinated stickers
- 6¾" x 7¼" pieces of patterned paper
- 6¾" x 7¼" transparencies
- bookplates
- brads
- 24" length of ribbon
- stamp pad
- chalk

TOOLS

- paper trimmer
- paper piercer
- craft knife
- self-healing cutting mat

ADHESIVE

- Xyron machine
- photo tabs

MATERIALS

gated album (7gypsies) • patterned paper, stickers (Pebbles Inc.) • pre-printed transparencies (Creative Imaginations, K&Company) • stamp pad (Ranger Industries) • brads (Making Memories) • bookplates (*twopeasinabucket.com*, Li'l Davis Designs) • ribbon (Offray) • American Typewriter font

Bertram & Minnie (Walton) Bills

I loved my great-grandparents and for a short time lived with them at my grandmother's house. gr. grandpop was near blind and we would listen to his books on tape together. He always went out of his way to make me feel special. He gave me one of his old pocket watches before he passed...I still have it.

paternal great grandparents and grandparents

Bertram & Charlotte (Betty) Bills

I called my grandfather "Pe-pop" to differentiate the 2 when I was young. Somehow ours was always an estranged relationship. After living with them a short time when my parents separated, we moved only a few miles away. They never called or visited and somehow expected me, a child, to continue the relationship. They were very cold people, this may explain a lot about my dad.

generations

single

succession

messages from beyond...believe it or not?

On the night and several days after my father passed, I experienced some very odd occurrences. Maybe I needed to believe in them or maybe they were coincidences, either way, I believe.
The night my father died my Uncle Donald, my father's brother called and blatantly proclaimed, "Your dad died." end of conversation. I was devastated by the news because I had recently tried to purge my feelings to him in a tape that was returned to me and felt he died before I told him how I felt. That night I received a mysterious phone call...the man on the other end said, "I just wanted you to know that your father loved you and I am toasting him with a rum and coke." and the phone went dead. My mom came upstairs and I told her what happened. I asked her what she was drinking she said, "rum & coke." The next night Raymond, childhood friend, and I were playing with the Ouija board and without prompting it began spelling out, "died before I had the chance to say I love you." We kept asking, "Who is this?" It repetitively spelled out " "D-A-D-D-A-D-D-A-D" Raymond and I just starred at each other in horror and vowed never to touch the Ouija board again.

Abbondi

Story has according to arranged to successful DeNave. Howeve he was kille Brooklyn, NY wed. This le marry the next

Having her hea of Joe, Abbor simple man, bring home st exactly what for her

They were marr Catholic Churc in 1928 and be Anthony, Jo

Abbon
born Sep
died Au

Angelina
born Dec
died Feb

gated album step-by-step

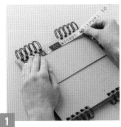

STEP ONE

Place sticker strips on left and right sides of gated cover. Print title on cardstock, cut to 5¾" x 7½". *Note: Check the spacing and make sure the gatefold opening will not open through any words.*

STEP TWO

Ink cardstock edges and apply gray chalk (see "Chalking" on p. 219).

STEP THREE

Adhere title page to left-side cover; right half of title page will hang over.

STEP FOUR

Trim off right half of title page and adhere to right-side cover.

STEP FIVE

To create album pages, cut random pages in half, using a paper trimmer.

STEP SIX

Print journaling on cardstock. Ink edges, and adhere to pages.

STEP SEVEN

Adhere patterned paper to section pages, e.g., "Legacy," "Childhood," and "School Days." Attach transparencies over patterned paper, using bookplates and brads.

STEP EIGHT

Embellish pages using photos and stickers.

STEP NINE

Tie off album by threading ribbon between the back cover and last page of the album. Tie in front.

Helpful Tips

Choose a color scheme and embellishments that won't compete with your photos, and keep them the same throughout the album. To maintain a consistent design, try adding a sticker strip down the sides of each full page.

Working with a pre-made album requires a little more planning. Create a framework for the theme and subjects you wish to include and decide how many pages you need to allot for each. For example, my framework includes:

- **Family legacy**—family photos and stories
- **Childhood journey**—favorite photos and stories of my childhood from my mother's perspective
- **School days**—school photos and sentiments, plus a series of prom photos and fashions (eek)
- **College years**—a collection of photos and stories describing my life post-high school, including the story of how I met my husband
- **Memorabilia**—report cards, miscellaneous photos, etc.

my travels

CANVAS MAT BOARD ALBUM

Moved by the art and architecture I had seen from my travels in Europe, I wanted to find the perfect canvas from which to create a small travel album. While browsing the art aisles of my local craft store, I found packs of canvas mat boards. I embellished each one with photos and journaling from each city I visited, and tied them all together with ribbon and a handle to remind me of a little suitcase.

SUPPLIES

- six 5" x 7" canvas mat boards
- acrylic paint
- rub-on letters and numbers
- large alphabet stamps

- six 5" x 7" pieces of white cardstock
- solvent-based stamp pad
- five metal-rimmed tags with jump rings

- five small bulldog clips
- two 12" lengths of ribbon
- drawer handle

TOOLS

- paper trimmer
- hand drill and large drill bit
- foam brushes
- pencil and eraser
- scissors

ADHESIVE

- Xyron machine
- dots

MATERIALS

paint, metal-rimmed tags, rub-on letters (Making Memories) • ribbon (Offray) • rub-on dates (Autumn Leaves) • rubber stamps (Limited Edition Rubberstamps, Green Pepper Press) • stamp pad (Tsukineko) • hand drill (Fiskars)

canvas mat board album **step-by-step**

STEP ONE

Brush two colors of acrylic paint across the front of each canvas mat board. Let dry.

STEP TWO

Use stamps or rub-ons to create the album title on one mat board. Set aside.

STEP THREE

On remaining mat boards, use stamps and rub-ons to add titles. *Note: Leave room for photos.* Adhere photos with dots.

STEP FOUR

For the back of each page, handwrite or print journaling on cardstock. *Note: I set my margins in Microsoft Word, printed my text on 8½" x 11", and trimmed.*

STEP FIVE

Lightly paint edges of cardstock. Create a "paint frame" by gently sweeping edges of brush along pencil marks. Let dry.

STEP SIX

Add photos and adhere cardstock pages to back of canvas boards.

STEP SEVEN

Drill two holes in mat boards for binding and handle, approx. 2" from the sides, and ⅜" from the spine (see "Craft hand drill" on p. 215).

STEP EIGHT

Place photos in "paint frames."

STEP NINE

To embellish, place rub-on dates on metal-rimmed tags. Thread jump rings through holes of bulldog clips and place clips over photos on the front pages.

STEP TEN

Thread ribbons through the holes of all six mat boards. Thread through holes of handle and tie in bows. *Note: Make knot large enough so ribbon does not slip through. Use ribbon that is at least ¾" wide to secure the weight of the canvas mat boards.*

what do you do all day?

POST-BOUND ALBUM

There's more to life than milestones—there's the everyday activities that form the bulk of existence. So I filled this 6" x 12" post-bound album with random snapshots of my day: hanging out in the backyard with the kids, going to the movies, picking strawberries. For added flair, I included large tags between each page protector to allow extra space for more photos—and more opportunities to celebrate the little things.

SUPPLIES

- 6" x 12" post-bound album
- 6" lengths of assorted wire-edged ribbons
- 10 6¼" x 3⅛" manila tags
- stamp pad

- 20 6" x 12" pieces of cardstock, various colors
- 20 4" x 6" pieces of cardstock, various colors

TOOLS

- paper trimmer with scoring blade
- labeler

ADHESIVE

- double-sided adhesive tape

MATERIALS

post-bound album (Westrim) • tags (DMD, Inc.) • labeler (Dymo) • ribbon (Offray) • stamp pad (Ranger Industries) • Arial font

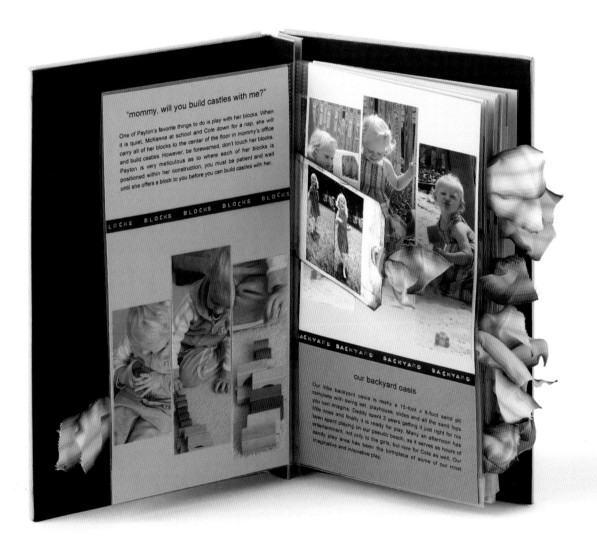

post-bound album step-by-step

STEP ONE
Print or write text on 4" x 6" piece of cardstock. Adhere to top or bottom of 6" x 12" page.

STEP TWO
Create 6" word strip, using labeler, and adhere across the width of the page where the two cardstock pieces meet.

STEP THREE
Trim three portrait-oriented photos to a size slightly smaller than 6" x 2". Adhere to page.

STEP FOUR
Print or write text on one side of tag.

STEP FIVE
Ink edges (see "Inking" on p. 219), and tie ribbon through tag hole.

STEP SIX
Trim additional photos and adhere to tag. *Note: You can use one, two or three small, individual photos on the tag, or use a multi-lens camera such as the Lomographic Pop 9 or Lomographic Supersampler.*

STEP SEVEN
Score tags ¾" from bottom, and adhere to the seam of page protectors using double-sided tape. *Note: Vary the placement of your tags.*

Helpful Tip

For a minimum investment, you can purchase multi-lens cameras that offer new photo options. The Lomographic Pop 9 takes nine identical pictures of your subject simultaneously while the Lomographic Supersampler takes four shots in quick sequence on a single photo. For more information on lomographic photography, see *shop.lomography.com*.

circle of friends

BLUE JEAN CHIPBOARD ALBUM

There are two things a woman should never take for granted: the fit of a comfy pair of jeans and the company of good friends. With this in mind, I created this scrapbook to celebrate the friendships I have made with some spectacular women. The album was passed among nine of my friends, each of whom completed her own two-page spread before passing it along. It's an amazing keepsake, and a story of the journeys we have taken along the road of friendship.

SUPPLIES

- two 8" x 7" pieces of cardboard
- two 10" x 9" pieces of patterned paper
- 11 8" x 7" pieces of chipboard
- two 8" pieces of leather cording
- pair of old jeans

- rub-on letters
- foam alphabet stamps
- acrylic paint
- four ³⁄₁₆" eyelets

TOOLS

- paper trimmer
- fabric scissors
- foam brush
- eyelet-setting tools
- hand drill and largest drill bit

ADHESIVE

- two double-sided adhesive sheets
- Xyron machine
- photo tabs

MATERIALS

patterned paper (7gypsies, SEI, Chatterbox) • rub-ons, foam stamps, acrylic paint, eyelets, leather flowers, brads, mailbox letters, metal-rimmed tag (Making Memories) • hand drill (Fiskars) • woven label (me & my BIG ideas) • filmstrip (Creative Imaginations) •stamp pad (Ranger Industries) • ribbon (Offray) • Attic Antique and Caslon Regular fonts

blue jean chipboard album step-by-step

STEP ONE

Cover cardboard with 10" x 9" sheets of patterned paper (see "Wrapping Chipboard Covers" on p. 218).

STEP TWO

Trim jeans around back pocket to measure 8¼" x 7¼". Trim another 8¼" x 7¼" section from jean's leg. Adhere denim to uncovered side of cardboard, using adhesive sheet. Press firmly, then trim off any excess denim hanging over edges.

STEP THREE

Use rub-on letters for "circle of" and stamp "friends" with acrylic paint.

STEP FOUR

Drill two holes through covers, about 1½" from top and bottom, and ½" from spine. Drill holes through chipboard pages at same spots (see "Craft hand drill" on p. 215).

STEP FIVE

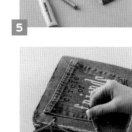

Set eyelets in covers. *Note: Eyelets will not completely reach through the cardboard because of its thickness, so use a hammer and setter to force eyelet ends into the sides of cardboard (see "Setting Eyelets" on p. 219).*

STEP SIX

Thread each piece of leather cording through covers and pages. Tie to bind. Send album to first participant!

STEP SEVEN

To create pages, untie binding and remove chipboard pages. Adhere papers, photos, and embellishments directly to chipboard and punch holes for binding. Rethread page to reassemble.

Helpful Tip

The number of chipboard pages you make will vary depending on the number of participants in the album. Just be sure to include enough pages for everyone to create her entries.

SHE WAS JUST THIS NAME,

in the beginning. Donna Downey. Fabulous alliteration. Whether she could scrapbook or not wasn't even the point. But she could. I saw her layouts on Two Peas, and was instantly sending links to my compadres at Simple Scrapbooks. "Check this girl out!" And they did. And the rest is history. | I think we e-mailed in the beginning. It's weird, because it kind of feels like I've known her forever. She is my "I get to be completely myself" friend in the scrapbook industry. I can let my hair down, so to speak, around Donna. It's something that's vitally important to me because sometimes, I feel like I can't always let the real me come out, if you get my drift. And so, I have D. She is far more creative than anyone I know and yet really doesn't take credit for her talent. Humble. That's the word. She does things I wouldn't even dream of. And it's inspiring. She is my friend and confidant and I wouldn't be having as much fun in this whole "thing" without her. Cheers, D. You rock, and you know it. Love, Cathy

DC

a true friend

COIN ENVELOPE ALBUM

With almost 20 years of friendship between us, my friend Karen and I have plenty of stories to tell, and lots of secrets to keep. I made this little scrapbook, using ordinary office supply coin envelopes as pages, to tell our own story—from the laughter to the tears to the experiences that have shaped our lives. Hidden inside each envelope are special sentiments and secrets.

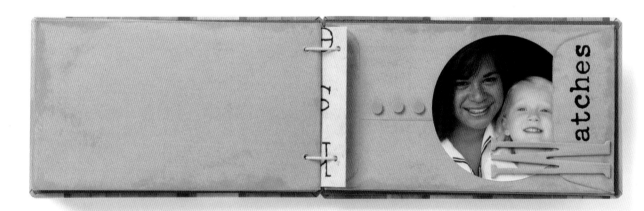

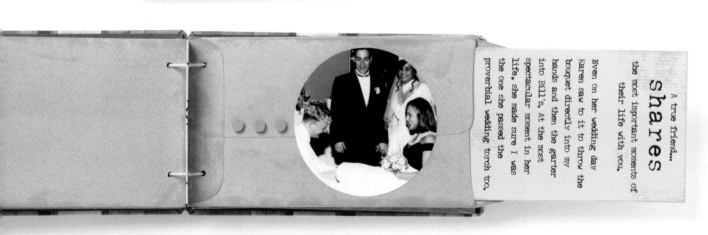

coin envelope album step-by-step

STEP ONE
Wrap 5¾" x 8¼" pieces of patterned paper over chipboard (see "Wrapping Chipboard Covers" p. 218).

STEP TWO
To create the accordion spine, adhere two 3¼" x 12" strips back to back so that the patterned sides face out. Repeat with two more strips.

STEP THREE
Accordion-fold each strip every ¾", and adhere the two strips together. Trim your accordion so that you have 12 valleys. *Note: The envelopes will sit in each valley.*

STEP FOUR
Adhere front and back covers to the ends of the accordion, making sure everything is centered.

STEP FIVE
Adhere 6" x 3½" cardstock pieces to the undersides of each cover to hide the unfinished edges.

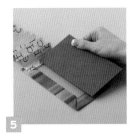

STEP SIX
Ink 10 coin envelopes (see "Inking" on p. 219). Place (do *not* adhere) and center one coin envelope in each valley of the accordion.

STEP SEVEN
Drill two holes approx. ¾" from the top and bottom and ⅜" from the end. Drill through the entire spine including covers, folds, and envelopes (see "Craft hand drill" on p. 215).

STEP EIGHT
Set eyelets in front and back covers. *Note: Eyelet end may not reach all the way through chipboard, so place the setter in the underside hole and hit with a hammer to secure the eyelet.*

STEP NINE
Thread elastic up from the back cover to the front cover through the metal-rimmed tag and down through the other side.

STEP TEN
Use circle punch to cut out photos. Adhere to pages. Embellish album using rub-ons and stencil letters. *Note: Paint one stencil letter for each envelope. Use a hand punch to punch small circles from the unused portion of the stencil and place next to photo.*

STEP ELEVEN
Print journaling (see "Printing Journaling" on p. 220) on cardstock and place in envelopes.

family

ENVELOPE ACCORDION ALBUM

This album is dear to my heart. Layered inside each envelope is a personal story to my children reflecting on the joys of motherhood and our family. Albums like this make great keepsakes, and in some ways they're therapeutic, too. It's a chance to tell my kids those things I'd always wanted to say—if only they'd sit still long enough to listen.

envelope accordion album step-by-step

STEP ONE
Cover chipboard with 7½" x 9¼" patterned paper (see "Wrapping Chipboard Covers" on p. 218).

STEP TWO
To create accordion spine, adhere two 5¾" x 12" patterned paper strips back to back, so that the patterned sides face out.

STEP THREE
Accordion-fold strip lengthwise every 1", using bone folder.

STEP FOUR
Cut four envelopes from corrugated paper. *Note: You can use regular cardstock.* Score and fold envelope flaps.

STEP FIVE
Open envelope and lay flat. Use anywhere hole punch and hammer to punch hole through larger envelope flaps (centered lengthwise). Attach button snaps through holes. Repeat for remaining three envelopes. *Note: Instead of button snaps, set an eyelet through the center of a small circle of cardstock.*

STEP SIX
Lay out accordion-folded strip so that the two ends point up.

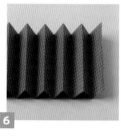

STEP SEVEN
In the second valley, adhere envelope to the right side. *Note: Be sure the envelope is centered top-to-bottom within the valley.* Secure with three eyelets. Repeat above step for remaining three envelopes, adhering envelopes in the third, fourth and fifth valleys.

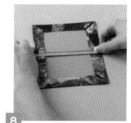

STEP EIGHT
Adhere ribbon across inside back cover.

STEP NINE
In the first valley in the back, adhere back cover to the right side. In the first valley in the front, adhere front cover to the left side.

STEP TEN
Adhere cardstock pieces to inside front and back covers.

STEP ELEVEN
Embellish envelopes with journaling and photos. Attach tag, transparency, and flower to smaller flaps with brads (see photo on p. 55).

STEP TWELVE
Use sheer ribbon to close envelopes with button snap closures.

favorite family photos 2004

Sometimes after I finish an album, I'm so darn proud of how it turned out that I want to make one for everyone I know. But I just don't have that kind of time—or stamina. Thank goodness someone at Shutterfly, an online photo service, was smart enough to come up with this stylish, cost-effective solution. Upload some photos, type in some journaling, and everyone can get a copy. Plus, your sanity remains intact.

SUPPLIES
- two 2' lengths of ribbon
- photos, either traditional or digital

TOOLS
- computer with Internet access

ADHESIVE
- none

MATERIALS
shutterfly.com • ribbon (Making Memories, Offray)

McKenna

First day of school, St.
Mark 4-year old
Pre-school

dramatic, whimsical,
wide-open, funny,
intelligent, beautiful
and loving

All grown up, I swear she
changes everyday. Our
high-spirited tomboy that
rejects all that is pink and
frilly has had a great
year. She has learned to
write her name, recognize
simple words like "stop" and
"no" and has grown
incredibly independent.

shutterfly photo album step-by-step

STEP ONE
Visit *shutterfly.com* and establish an account by clicking "Sign up." *Note: There is no charge to open an account.*

STEP TWO
Click "Shutterfly Store."

STEP THREE
Click "Photo Books" on left side of screen.

STEP FOUR
Click "Get started." Select black suede cover. Click "Next." Select simple style. Click "Next." *Note: Choose from a variety of album covers, colors, styles, and layouts. The hardcover books measure 8¾" x 11¼" and the soft cover books measure 5½" x 7½".*

STEP FIVE
To complete the album, follow the simple, step-by-step prompts and instructions. *Note: It takes about a week to receive the album in the mail.*

STEP SIX
Wrap ribbon around front cover and tie (see photo on p. 57).

Helpful Tips

If you've been leery of digital scrapbooking, then fear no more! Shutterfly walks you through every step. I couldn't believe how easy it was. And the album looks like a professionally published book. You can have up to six photos per page with the larger, hardcover books, or four photos per page with the smaller, softcover books. And the albums make perfect baby or wedding gifts. Don't forget to incorporate a few journaling captions into your Shutterfly design. Some heartfelt sentences will make the book more meaningful.

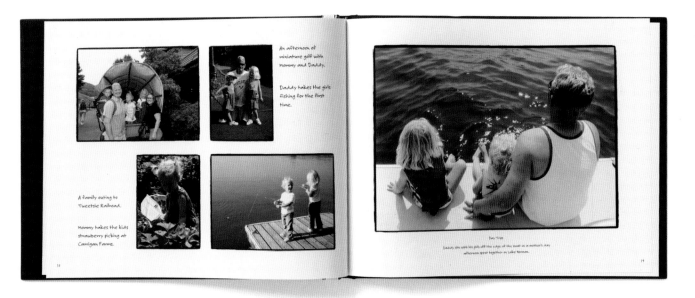

soccer 2004

FLIP-FLOP ACCORDION ALBUM

This past fall I lugged kids, snacks, and camera to my daughter's soccer games, and by the end of the season I'd accumulated dozens of photos. The season was even more special because Daddy was McKenna's first coach. To highlight the two-fold importance of this experience, I created a flip-flop accordion album. If you think you have flipped all the way through the album, keep flipping—there's a whole new story on the other side.

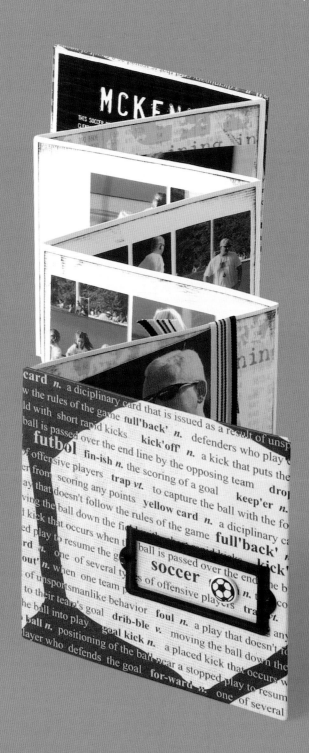

flip-flop accordion album **step-by-step**

STEP ONE

Wrap chipboard with patterned paper (see "Wrapping Chipboard Covers" on p. 218).

STEP TWO

Place bookplate on cover. Use paper piercer and push pad to create holes for brads. Secure bookplate with brads. Set soccer ball eyelet.

STEP THREE

Fold each 6" x 12" strip of cardstock in half lengthwise, and reopen to a "mountain" shape.

STEP FOUR

Adhere insides of two mountains to create a "Z" shape.

STEP FIVE

Attach inside of a third mountain to inside of second mountain. Repeat with fourth, fifth, and sixth pieces.

STEP SIX

Adhere front cover, making sure it opens to the left. Turn the album over and adhere back cover (it should also open to the left).

STEP SEVEN

Print journaling in reverse text on two pieces of 5¾" x 5¾" white cardstock (see "Printing Reverse Text" on p. 220). Adhere journaling pages to chipboard covers, covering the unfinished edges.

STEP EIGHT

Ink edges of remaining 5¾" x 5¾" pieces of white cardstock. Adhere each piece to front and backs of all 10 inside panels.

STEP NINE

Use photo tabs to adhere transparency sheets to four of the panels. *Note: Put tabs in the center of the transparencies so the photos will hide the adhesive.*

STEP TEN

Place photos throughout the album. Use clear stickers, rub-on date, ribbon, and metal-rimmed tag to finish album.

a lifetime of memories

ROLODEX ALBUM

I wanted to scrapbook umpteen boxes of not-so-great holiday photos without spending 10 years doing it. The Rolodex album is my solution. Not only am I scrapbooking dozens of sub-par photos that I just can't throw away, I'm also reducing the guilt associated with my failure to scrapbook all those events. So go through your boxes of photos and pull out one photo from each event you planned on scrapbooking—you'll be surprised how liberating it can be.

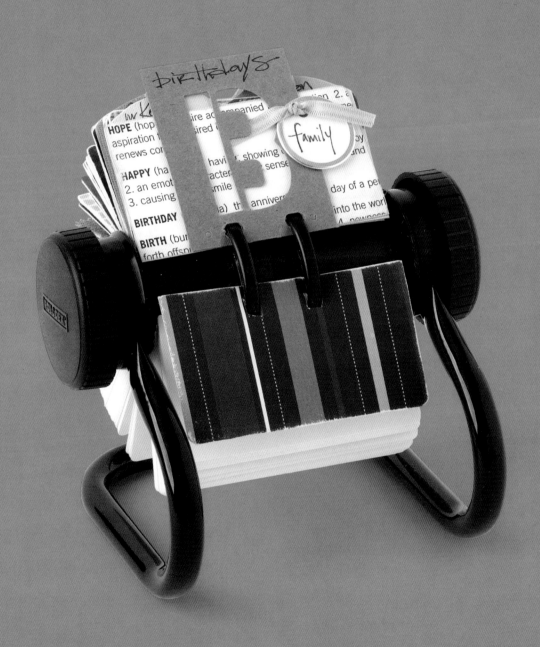

SUPPLIES

- 2¼" x 4" rotary card file (Rolodex)
- black marker
- rub-on numbers
- alphabet stencils
- assorted patterned papers
- 6" lengths of assorted ribbon
- assorted themed charms and tags
- 3" x 4" pieces of cardstock

TOOLS

- sanding block
- Rolodex punch
- scissors
- paper trimmer

ADHESIVE

- Xyron machine

MATERIALS

patterned paper (Chatterbox, Karen Foster Design, me & my BIG ideas, 7gypsies) • definition sticker, metal-rimmed tags (Making Memories) • rub-on numbers (KI Memories, Autumn Leaves, Creative Imaginations, Scrapworks) • charms (K&Company) • ribbon (Making Memories, May Arts, Offray) • marker (Sakura)

2003· On your 3ᴿᵈ birthday, you wanted to make your own Happy Birthday cake. We went to the store i you picked out your mix & icing all by yourself. You even bought m&m's to cover your cake in.

rolodex album step-by-step

STEP ONE
Trim each photo to 2¼" x 4" and adhere to a card. Trim overhanging edges with scissors. *Note: For a weathered look, use a sanding block to file edges.*

STEP TWO
Punch holes in photos, using the holes in the card as a guide.

STEP THREE
Add journaling to the back of the card and embellish photos with rub-ons.

STEP FOUR
Using patterned paper instead of photos, repeat Steps 1 and 2 to cover several cards.

STEP FIVE
To create event dividers, punch holes in bottom of alphabet stencil. Embellish with ribbon and charms or tags. Place paper covered cards behind stencil dividers.

STEP SIX
To create other dividers, adhere a 3" x 4" piece of cardstock to one side of Rolodex divider. Trim excess cardstock around divider and punch holes. Repeat with second piece of card-stock on other side of divider. Label with marker.

STEP SEVEN
File photo cards under appropriate theme, e.g., birthdays, Christmas, and school.

2002- by your 2nd birthday you
were old enough to pick out your
own outfit. Mr. Balloony man
had left you a big bunch of
balloons on the deck and you
were running around the
yard with them.

through the years

4" X 6" PHOTO ALBUM

My family's favorite place for Sunday breakfast is Bob Evans Restaurant. While we wait to be seated, I like to slip away to the gift shop and read the *In the Year You Were Born* cards. They describe what the world was like in a given year—the popular tunes, TV shows, and events, etc., that defined the times. This album is inspired by those cards, and is a miniaturized chronicle of facts, trivia, and pop culture documenting each year of my life.

SUPPLIES

- 4" x 6" photo album
- several pieces of 4" x 6¼" cardstock
- five pieces of coordinating colored cardstock
- leather flowers
- mini brads
- number stickers

TOOLS

- paper trimmer
- paper piercer or push pin
- push pad

ADHESIVE

- photo tabs

MATERIALS

4" x 6" photo album (Target) • stickers (Sticker Studio) • leather flowers (Making Memories) • brads (Bazzill Basics Paper) • Gill Sans, Helvetica Narrow Bold, and American Typewriter fonts

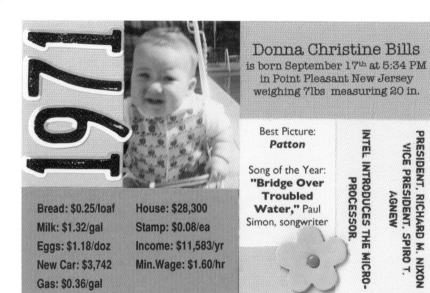

1971

Donna Christine Bills is born September 17th at 5:34 PM in Point Pleasant New Jersey weighing 7lbs measuring 20 in.

Best Picture:
Patton

Song of the Year:
"Bridge Over Troubled Water," Paul Simon, songwriter

INTEL INTRODUCES THE MICRO-PROCESSOR.

PRESIDENT, RICHARD M. NIXON
VICE PRESIDENT, SPIRO T. AGNEW

Bread: $0.25/loaf
Milk: $1.32/gal
Eggs: $1.18/doz
New Car: $3,742
Gas: $0.36/gal

House: $28,300
Stamp: $0.08/ea
Income: $11,583/yr
Min.Wage: $1.60/hr

1986

first serious boyfriend
bob haircut
getting my hair frosted
pooka shell necklaces
blue eyeliner and frosted pink lips
Esprit clothes were all the rage

LA GEAR
OP (OCEAN PACIFIC) CLOTHING
RAINBOW BRIGHT
AIR JORDAN'S
VANNA WHITE ON WHEEL OF FORTUNE

Best Picture:
Out of Africa

Song of the Year:
"We Are the World," Michael Jackson and Lionel Richie, songwriters

Space shuttle Challenger explodes after launch at Cape Canaveral, Fla., killing all seven aboard.

The Oprah Winfrey Show hits national television.

Nintendo video games introduced in U.S.

BEGINNING OF SOPHMORE YEAR ST. ROSE HS

4" x 6" photo album step-by-step

STEP ONE
Sketch a color-blocking template on a 4" x 6¼" piece of cardstock. *Note: Each opposing page is a mirror image of the template, so you only have to create one template (see photo on p. 67).*

STEP TWO
Trace and cut cardstock blocks and one photo to size, using template.

STEP THREE
Print text on cardstock blocks. *Note: Measure block sizes and create text boxes accordingly (see "Printing Journaling" on p. 220). Save your text box document to use for remaining pages. To print on blocks, see "Printing Text on Tags" on p. 220.*

STEP FOUR
Arrange and adhere blocks on a clean piece of 4" x 6¼" cardstock. *Note: Don't adhere on your template.* Use number stickers for year.

STEP FIVE
Attach one leather flower with brad per two-page spread, using a paper piercer and push pad to create guide hole.

STEP SIX
Repeat for each page.

Helpful Tip
Looking for info to include on your pages? Try these websites:

infoplease.com/yearbyyear.html

vh1.com

fun4birthdays.com/year/index.html

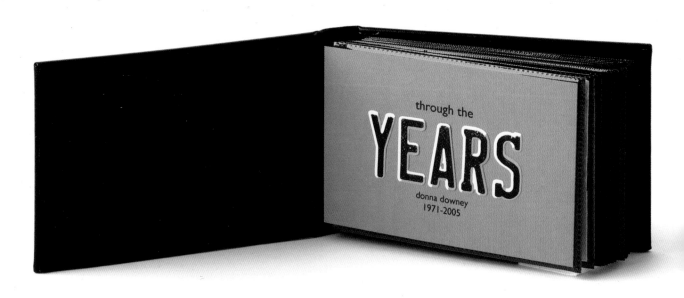

family recipes

BINDER BOARD ALBUM

It's really no secret that I do not know how to cook. Don't get me wrong, I do try, but thank goodness I married a man who is willing to eat just about anything I put down in front of him. So I started compiling an album of favorite family recipes. I asked family members to send me his or her favorite recipe along with a story or anecdote as to why it's a favorite; how could I go wrong, I figured, with a resource like this?

SUPPLIES

- nine 12" x 12" patterned papers and cardstock
- five 12" x 12" pieces of chipboard
- white spray paint
- binder spine
- 6¼" x 13¼" x ½" plywood
- bookplate and two screws
- white cardstock
- alphabet rub-ons
- two eyelet snaps
- stamp pad

TOOLS

- paper trimmer
- pencil
- hand-held hole punch
- screwdriver
- eyelet-setting tools
- sanding block

ADHESIVE

- Xyron machine
- photo tabs

MATERIALS

binder spine (Scrapbooks 'N More) • patterned paper (Chatterbox) • alphabet rub-ons (Autumn Leaves) • bookplate (Creative Imaginations) • eyelet snaps (Making Memories) • Helvetica font • stamp pad (Ranger Industries)

binder board album step-by-step

STEP ONE
Create cascading section pages from chipboard, each measuring 5¼" wide and ¾" shorter than the previous page. *Note: The page lengths should be 12", 11¼", 10½", 9¾", 9", 8¼", 7½", 6¾" and 6".*

STEP TWO
Cut two pieces, measuring the same as in Step 1, from each of the nine papers. Adhere one piece to the front and another to the back of each chipboard page. *Note: Do not wrap chipboard pages.*

STEP THREE
Before punching holes in chipboard pages, make a template on a piece of scrap paper to ensure that pages will fit loosely on binder spine. Punch holes in chipboard pages, using template as a guide. *Note: Save template to use with filler pages.*

STEP FOUR
Spray-paint plywood, binder spine, and bookplate. Let dry. Center and attach binder spine to board base with two screws.

STEP FIVE
Print "Family Recipes" on 1¼" x 2¾" piece of cardstock. Place bookplate over title and attach to cover, using two eyelet snaps (see "Setting Eyelets" on p. 219).

STEP SIX
Add section titles to bottom of chipboard pages, using alphabet rub-ons.

STEP SEVEN
Cut filler pages from cardstock to measure 5" wide and ¾" shorter than each of the lengths listed in Step 1. Ink edges. Print or write recipe and journaling.

STEP EIGHT
For opposing page, add pieces of inked patterned paper and photo. Punch holes and insert filler pages between coordinating section pages.

STEP NINE
Sand edges of section pages (see "Sanding" on p. 221).

Helpful Tip
Avoid using a decoupage adhesive such as Mod Podge for this album. The liquid adhesive may cause the chipboard pages to warp.

confessions of a shopaholic

SHOPPING BAG ALBUM

I just can't pass up a sale. So while browsing the aisles of my local craft store, I found a bundle of these inexpensive brown craft bags and tossed them into my shopping cart. I figured they were versatile enough for almost anything, and I kept them with my stash of other impulse purchases. Several weeks later I ran across them again, and I realized…it's a scrapbook!

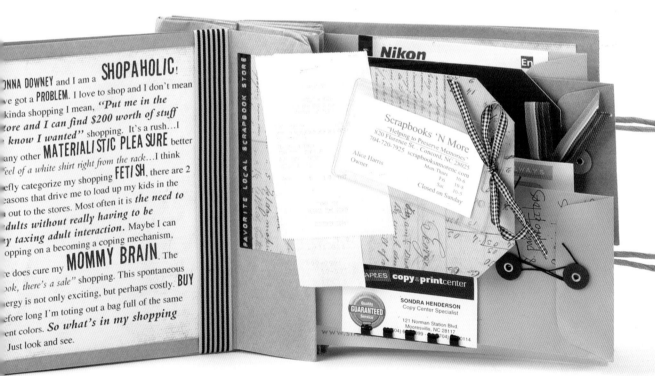

shopping bag album step-by-step

STEP ONE
Lay bag on flat surface with bottom flap showing. Fold bottom flap down towards the bottom of the bag so it creates a "Y" shape at the bottom. Repeat with another bag.

STEP TWO
Cut off bags 2" above the bottom flap. Discard tops.

STEP THREE
Layer the cut bottom portions, one on top of the other, so that you have four fanned flaps. Adhere cut sides together.

STEP FOUR
Lay an uncut bag on flat surface so that the bottom of the bag is not showing. Adhere bag bottom to the 2" portion of the cut bags.

STEP FIVE
Turn the entire album over and adhere another uncut bag to the back along the 2" portion of the cut bags.

STEP SIX
Using your prong fasteners as guides, mark where the four holes will be drilled for binding. Drill or punch holes through all four bags and bind with fasteners.

STEP SEVEN
To create the inner pages, adhere various envelopes, large tags, or cardstock pieces within the inner flaps.

STEP EIGHT
Print or write journaling on both 8" x 7½" pieces of cardstock. Ink edges and adhere to front and back inside covers. Place metal trim on left side of cardstock.

STEP NINE
Embellish pages using ribbon, photos, stickers, and charms. *Note: Don't forget to open the bag handles and insert memorabilia, newspaper ads, or more journaling.*

STEP TEN
To create the cover, use reverse text printing (see "Printing Reverse Text" on p. 220). Wrap ribbon around front cover. Tie in bow.

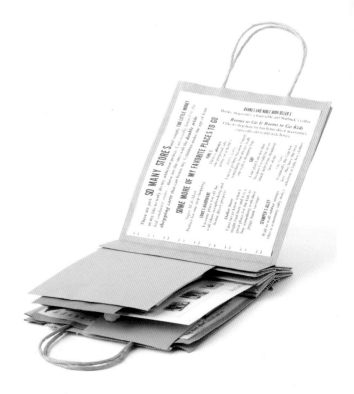

love

MINI-BOX ACCORDION ALBUM

Everyone loves a little box. People like to pick them up and cradle them for a second or two before opening the lid. Heck, these things beg to be handled. This one has a surprise, though—an accordion fold commemorating the bond between my husband and me. But really it could be about anything, so think outside the box (or should I say inside the box?).

mini-box accordion step-by-step

STEP ONE
Accordion-fold each strip of cardstock every 2¼". Trim off any partial accordion pages.

STEP TWO
Adhere accordion strips together by placing the last page of the first accordion strip on top of the first page of the second accordion strip. *Note: To create a longer album, simply add more accordion strips.*

STEP THREE
Adhere patterned squares to each page. Place photos, rub-on letters and words, and remaining embellishments on pages.

STEP FOUR
Adhere back of first page to inside of box lid. Adhere back of last page to inside of box base.

STEP FIVE
Place sticker on box lid.

cole

5¼" FLOPPY DISK ALBUM

Bette McIntyre, one of my loyal scrapbook students, pulled me aside one night after class and whipped a 5¼" floppy disk from her bag. "I have six boxes of these darn things sitting in my closet," she said. "Do you think you can do something with them?" The creative gears in my head immediately started to turn, and before you could say "obsolete technology," I'd come up with this nifty little scrapbook. If you can't get your hands on a box of 5¼" floppies, chipboard will do just as well.

SUPPLIES

- eight 5¼" floppy disks or 5¼" chipboard squares
- eight 5¼" x 5¼" pieces of coordinated, patterned paper
- eight 5¼" x 5¼" pieces of cardstock
- 12"–15" length of beaded chain
- letter stickers

TOOLS

- paper trimmer
- large circle template
- swivel knife and mat
- sanding block

ADHESIVE

- Xyron machine

MATERIALS

Coluzzle nested circle template, swivel knife, mat (Provo Craft) •
patterned paper (Basic Grey) • letter stickers (Sticker Studio) •
beaded chain (Making Memories) • American Typewriter font

floppy disk album step-by-step

STEP ONE

Use circle template (see "Cutting template" on p. 215), or trace hole in floppy disk, to cut small circles in the center of each 5¼" x 5¼" square of patterned paper. *Note: The Coluzzle nested circle template has eight circles to choose from. Use the second circle from the center for this project.*

STEP TWO

Adhere to one side of each disk.

STEP THREE

Print or write journaling on cardstock and adhere to the other side of each disk.
Note: To print journaling, create a 4¾" x 4¾" text box (see "Printing Journaling" on p. 220). Insert 1½" circle auto shape in the center of the text box to mark the placement of the hole in the floppy disk.

STEP FOUR

Trim seven photos to 1¾" x 5". Sand edges. Adhere each photo to seven of the disks. Add a title to each disk, using letter stickers.

STEP FIVE

To round corners and add a weathered look, sand edges of cardstock and patterned paper.

STEP SIX

Bind all pages with beaded chain.

The day that you first sat up is my favorite milestone. It seems like forever until an infant can finally sit up on their own and once they do, life seems to get just that much easier. Sitting up means that carrying and placing you down became so much easier, you now can play with toys from a better vantage point and we can all play games with you. From the moment you first sat up, you have had a toy car or truck in your hand. There is something about wheeling that toy across the floor that is so entertaining to you and you full body giggle as you manage to wheel it across the floor. Even more fun is to watch your face light up as the car is gently rolled back to you, bumping up against the tips of your toes. With each milestone you reach, I watch you change and grow into a little boy. These are the days I want to hold on to forever.

you-nique

CLIPBOARD ALBUM

My daughter Payton has this thing for shoes. She loves them all: sandals, sneakers, penny loafers, and boots. So I created this album from an inexpensive clipboard to showcase Payton's curious infatuation with shoes. By simply attaching a cover and filler pages to the altered clipboard, I have the perfect showcase for this amusing album.

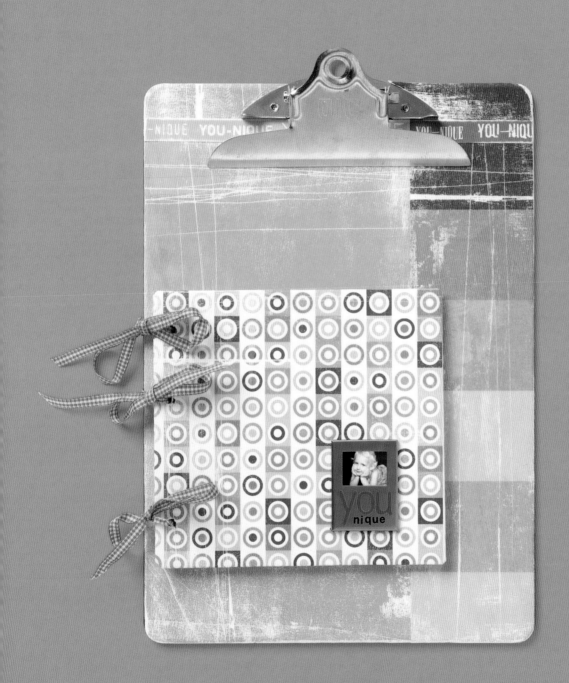

SUPPLIES

- letter size clipboard
- three 12" x 12" pieces of patterned paper
- 6½" x 6" piece of chipboard
- 5¾" x 6¼" piece of cardstock or patterned paper
- 10 6½" x 6" pieces of cardstock

- three 8" lengths of ribbon
- small metal frame
- letter rub-ons

TOOLS

- paper trimmer
- foam brush
- brayer
- craft knife
- sanding block
- bone folder
- hand drill and largest bit

ADHESIVE

- decoupage adhesive
- Xyron machine
- photo tabs

MATERIALS

patterned paper (Basic Grey) • frame (Scrapworks) • rub-ons (Scrapworks, Chartpak) • ribbon (Offray) • hand drill (Fiskars) • Arial Narrow font • decoupage adhesive (Plaid)

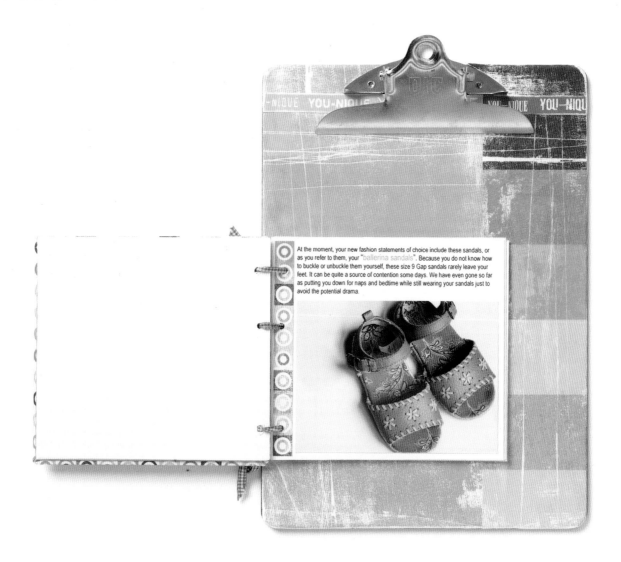

At the moment, your new fashion statements of choice include these sandals, or as you refer to them, your "ballerina sandals". Because you do not know how to buckle or unbuckle them yourself, these size 9 Gap sandals rarely leave your feet. It can be quite a source of contention some days. We have even gone so far as putting you down for naps and bedtime while still wearing your sandals just to avoid the potential drama.

clipboard album step-by-step

STEP ONE

Cut patterned paper to 6½" x 12" and 3½" x 1" pieces. Brush coat of decoupage adhesive on left side of clipboard and underneath clip. Place larger piece of paper on clipboard, top edge flush with clip base. Use brayer to smooth out air bubbles or creases.

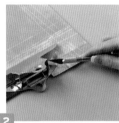

STEP TWO

Repeat Step 1 to cover top left-hand side of clipboard with smaller piece of paper. Trim around clip base, using craft knife. Let dry for 5 mins. Sand off excess edges.

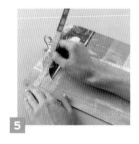

STEP THREE

Cut patterned paper to 3½" x 12" and 3½" x 1" pieces. Brush coat of decoupage adhesive on right side of clipboard and underneath clip. Place larger piece of paper on clipboard, top edge flush with clip base. Use brayer to smooth out air bubbles or creases.

STEP FOUR

Repeat Step 3 to cover top right-hand side of clipboard with smaller piece of paper. Trim around clip base, using craft knife. Let dry for 5 mins. Sand off excess edges.

STEP FIVE

Create a computer-generated word strip on patterned paper, using reverse text printing (see "Printing Reverse Text" on p. 220). Lift clip and adhere strip across board along paper seams.

STEP SIX

Cut patterned paper to 8½" x 8", and cover chipboard (see "Wrapping Chipboard Covers" on p. 218). Adhere 6¼" x 5¾" piece of cardstock or patterned paper to inside front cover.

STEP SEVEN

Embellish metal frame with rub-ons, insert photo, and place on album cover.

STEP EIGHT

Adhere one ½" x 5¾" strip of patterned paper to left side of each 6½" x 6" piece of cardstock. Complete album pages using photos and journaling.

STEP NINE

Stack pages and cover; place on clipboard. Drill three holes approx. ¾" from left edge of clipboard. Drill through cover, pages, and clipboard. *Note: You'll need to secure the clipboard with a clamp or have someone hold it in place while you drill.*

STEP TEN

Thread ribbon through holes and tie to clipboard.

decorative journals

home

THREE-RING BINDER JOURNAL

Sometimes it's more work to leave my children with a sitter than it is just to stay home. When I do have to travel, I feel more at ease when I leave this journal, affectionately referred to as "the binder," behind for my family. It's filled with important information like emergency numbers, favorite television channels, collections of take-out menus, and even a few all-powerful Barbie band-aids that seem to solve most any problem my children have.

SUPPLIES

- standard 1" three-ring binder
- two 9¾" x 12" pieces of patterned paper
- two 12" lengths of bookbinding tape
- five 8½" x 11" pieces of cardstock
- metal mailbox letters
- cardstock
- 12 eyelets
- 8½" x 11" page protectors

ADHESIVE

- decoupage adhesive
- Xyron machine or other double-sided adhesive

MATERIALS

patterned paper (Chatterbox) • bookbinding tape, mailbox letters, eyelets (Making Memories) • portable die-cut machine and index tab die (Sizzix) • Copperplate font

TOOLS

- paper trimmer
- foam brush
- brayer
- sanding block
- eyelet-setting tools
- portable die-cut machine
- 2¾" x 1½" rectangle index tab die
- three-hole punch

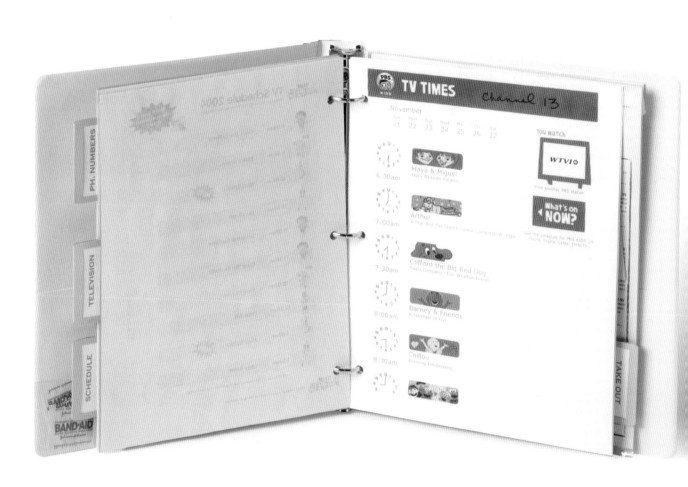

three-ring binder journal step-by-step

STEP ONE
Apply decoupage over entire front cover of binder. Starting at right edge of cover, adhere one piece of patterned paper. Smooth using brayer.

STEP TWO
Let dry 15 min. Use sanding block to remove excess paper edges.

STEP THREE
Repeat Steps 1 and 2 for back cover.

STEP FOUR
Starting at back cover, wrap one piece of bookbinding tape over patterned paper and around half of spine. Repeat with second piece of tape, wrapping over spine and front cover.

STEP FIVE
Print text on cardstock, and trim to 11½" x ⅝" (see "Printing Reverse Text" on p. 220). Adhere flush with edge of tape on front cover. Adhere letters over text strip.

STEP SIX
To create dividers, use three-hole punch to punch holes in left side of four cardstock pieces.

STEP SEVEN
Die-cut four tabs from cardstock. Print tab titles on separate pieces of cardstock and trim to fit inside tabs.

STEP EIGHT
Place tabs, in cascading positions, to right sides of 8½" x 11" cardstock pieces and secure with three eyelets per tab (see "Setting Eyelets" on p. 219). *Note: If you don't have a portable die-cut machine, you can use office index tabs.*

STEP NINE
Add pages of information behind dividers. *Note: Use page protectors to store menus or other documents.*

a reflection of family

CORRUGATED COVER JOURNAL

Family, although often separated by miles, is seldom separated in heart. Yet it can be difficult to keep up with the many milestones and accomplishments. That's why I turned a dollar journal into a keepsake that I'll initiate passing from one family member to the next. Inside is a one-of-a-kind story told by each member of my extended family sharing highlights of the past year. Simply cover the original journal exterior with your favorite papers, add some instructions inside, and wait for its return.

SUPPLIES

- 5¾" x 8¼" hard-bound journal
- two 6" x 10" pieces of patterned paper
- two 5½" x 8¼" pieces of corrugated cardstock
- 8½" length of book binding tape
- cardstock
- metal mailbox numbers
- paper flowers
- decorative brad
- two 24" lengths of ribbon

TOOLS

- paper trimmer
- bone folder
- scissors
- sanding block
- portable die-cut machine
- 1¼" x ¾" rectangle index tab die

ADHESIVE

- Xyron machine
- photo tabs
- dots

MATERIALS

patterned paper (7gypsies) • ribbon, metal mailbox numbers, paper flowers, mini-brads, decorative brad, book binding tape (Making Memories) • metal tag (K&Company) • portable die-cut machine and index tab die (Sizzix) • Optima and Dymo fonts

corrugated cover journal step-by-step

STEP ONE
Apply adhesive to surface of inside front cover. Place patterned paper flush with spine edge. Smooth paper over cover, allowing three remaining paper sides to extend past cover edges.

STEP TWO
Apply adhesive to extending edges of paper. Fold two corners over cover. Wrap three sides over cover.

STEP THREE
Repeat Steps 1 and 2 above for inside back cover.

STEP FOUR
Starting at right edge of front cover, adhere corrugated card-stock, making sure to leave ⅜" of spine exposed. Use sanding block to remove excess paper edges (see "Sanding" on p. 221). Repeat with back cover.

STEP FIVE
Wrap book binding tape around spine, over corrugated paper edges.

STEP SIX
Print journaling and instructions on cardstock and trim to 5½" x 8". Adhere to first page.

STEP SEVEN
Wrap ribbon around front cover, next to spine, and tie in bow.

STEP EIGHT
Print title on cardstock and trim to 4¾" x ½". Adhere to cover. Embellish cover with decorative brad and paper flowers, and mailbox numbers.

STEP NINE
Die-cut tabs from cardstock. Print tab titles on separate cardstock pieces and trim to fit inside tabs.

STEP TEN
Place tabs, in cascading positions, on journal pages, and secure with one eyelet per tab (see "Setting Eyelets" on p. 219). *Note: If you don't have a portable die-cut machine, you can use office index tabs.*

cherish

DVD TIN JOURNAL

"Hey, Donna, do you think you can do something cool with these?" asks Alice, my local scrapbook store owner, as she hands me a silver DVD tin. I'm quiet for a moment, then I grin with the possibilities. As I open the tin I realize it's hinged, I immediately determine, "It's gotta be a journal!" There's nothing like little concealed places to stow away ideas—and the fact that I can keep my pen inside and close it up, well, that's just icing on the cake!

SUPPLIES

- 7½" x 5¼" DVD tin
- 4⅞" x 6⅞" piece of cardstock (color 1)
- 4⅞" x 4" piece of cardstock (color 2)
- 4⅞" x 6⅞" piece of cardstock (color 2)
- 4⅞" x 4" piece of cardstock (color 1)
- 4⅞" x ¼" strip of patterned paper
- 1¼" circle of patterned paper
- two mini-brads
- three metal word charms
- large and small silk flowers
- two 2⅝" x 5¼" shipping tags
- two 6" lengths of ribbon
- 5" x 8" memo pad

TOOLS

- paper trimmer
- corner rounder
- hand drill and third-largest bit
- 1½" circle punch
- paper piercer
- hammer
- craft knife and ruler
- self-healing cutting mat

ADHESIVE

- Xyron machine
- double-sided tape

MATERIALS

DVD tin (Scrapbooks 'N More) • patterned paper (7gypsies) • word charms (K&Company) • mini-brads, ribbon (Making Memories) • tags (DMD, Inc.) • hand drill (Fiskars)

dvd tin journal step-by-step

STEP ONE
Round all four corners of 4⅞" x 6⅞" cardstock (color 1). Round bottom corners only of 4⅞" x 4" cardstock (color 2).

STEP TWO
Adhere smaller cardstock piece on top of larger cardstock piece, so that bottom rounded corners match up. Adhere to cover.

STEP THREE
Open tin. Drill hole for brad on cover over cardstock seam. Remove stems and centers from flowers. Punch 1¼" circle of patterned paper and pierce hole in center for brad.

STEP FOUR
Push and secure brad through word charm, patterned paper, large flower, and tin. Flip to underside of tin lid and lightly tap brad prongs flat with hammer.

STEP FIVE
Round all four corners of 4⅞" x 6⅞" cardstock (color 2). Round bottom corners only of 4⅞" x 4" cardstock (color 1).

STEP SIX
Place smaller cardstock piece on top of larger cardstock piece, so that bottom rounded corners match up. To create pocket, adhere sides and bottom only.

STEP SEVEN
Adhere strip of patterned paper to top edge of pocket. Adhere small flower and brad over strip.

STEP EIGHT
Embellish tags with ribbon and word charms. Place tags inside pocket.

STEP NINE
Use craft knife and ruler to trim memo pad to 5" x 7". *Note: I trimmed 6 to 8 pieces of memo paper at a time.* Place pad and pen inside tin.

you can

COVERED LEGAL PAD

With the power of positive thinking, transform an ordinary legal pad into a diary for goal-setting milestones. The cover is totally removable and transferable, so you only have to create it once. As you fill a pad, simply release the prong fasteners, remove the cover, and add it to a new pad.

SUPPLIES

- 8½" x 11¾" legal pad
- 5½" x 10½" piece of patterned paper
- 9" x 10½" piece of patterned paper
- 8½" x 10¾" piece of chipboard
- 1" x 8½" piece of chipboard
- 12" x ½" strip of patterned paper
- bookplate and two mini-brads
- bookcloth
- 8¼" x 11½" piece of cardstock
- two-piece prong fastener

TOOLS

- hand drill and largest bit
- paper trimmer
- paper piercer
- push pad
- two-hole punch or handheld hole punch
- pencil
- bone folder

ADHESIVE

- Xyron machine
- double-sided tape
- strips

MATERIALS

patterned paper (Diane's Daughters) • bookplate (Creative Imaginations) • mini-brads (Making Memories) • book cloth (Chatterbox) • hand drill (Fiskars)

covered legal pad step-by-step

STEP ONE
Adhere two patterned paper pieces lengthwise, overlapping ½", to create one large 14" x 10½" sheet.

STEP TWO
Apply adhesive to one side of both chipboard pieces. Center and adhere pieces to the back of patterned paper, making sure to leave a 1/16" space between the small and large piece.

STEP THREE
Apply strips of double-sided tape around entire perimeter. *Note: Treat chipboard pieces as one sheet.* Wrap patterned paper around chipboard (see "Wrapping Chipboard Covers" on p. 218).

STEP FOUR
Adhere 12" x ½" patterned paper strip to front of cover, over paper seam, and wrap ends around edges.

STEP FIVE
Print title on book cloth and adhere behind bookplate using glue strips. Position bookplate on cover. Pierce holes for brads and secure (see "Piercing Guide Holes" on p. 221.)

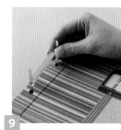

STEP SIX
Center and adhere cardstock to underside of chipboard cover.

STEP SEVEN
Slightly bend cover (where large and small chipboard pieces meet) to create crease.

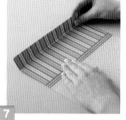

STEP EIGHT
Use two-hole punch to create holes through smaller chipboard piece for prong fastener. *Note: You can also use handheld hole punch.* Place punched cover over legal pad and mark placement for holes on pad.

STEP NINE
Drill holes through pad. Push prong fastener ends through holes in pad and cover, and fasten together.

kaleidoscope perspectives

SCRAPS JOURNAL

I am really good at accumulating scraps of cardstock, but really bad at going through them and reusing them. So in an effort to chip away at the mounting piles of scraps, I used them to create a colorful journal. I simply pulled out all the larger scraps to create the filler pages and used some of the smaller pieces to tear a kaleidoscope-like cover. I don't know about you, but I just love getting more for less!

SUPPLIES

- two 9" x 6" pieces of cardstock
- two 7" x 4" pieces of chipboard
- cardstock scraps
- 8½" x 11" piece of cardstock
- bookplate
- two eyelets
- two 6¾" x 3¾" pieces of cardstock
- 30-50 4" x 7" pieces of cardstock

TOOLS

- paper trimmer
- bone folder
- eyelet-setting tools
- pencil
- paper piercer

ADHESIVE

- Xyron machine
- glue stick

MATERIALS

bookplate (Creative Imaginations) • eyelets (Making Memories) •
4990810 font

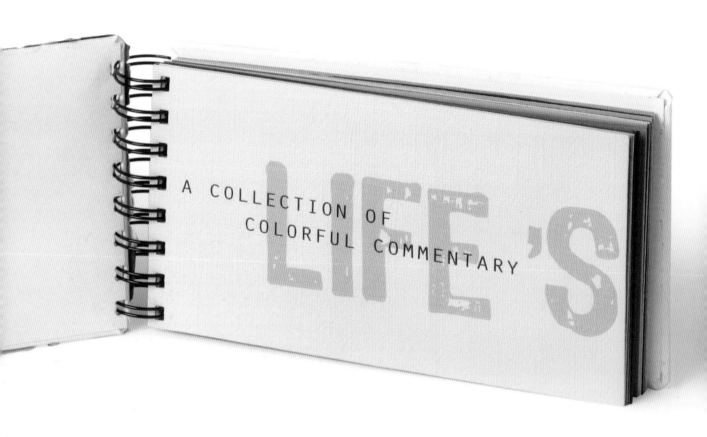

scraps journal step-by-step

STEP ONE
Use 9" x 6" cardstock pieces to cover chipboard pieces (see "Wrapping Chipboard Covers" on p. 218). *Note: Use bone folder to help wrap cardstock around chipboard.*

STEP TWO
Tear small pieces from cardstock scraps. Use glue stick to adhere pieces randomly to front cover.

STEP THREE
Print cover title on 8½" x 11" cardstock and trim to fit behind bookplate. Position bookplate on cover, and mark holes for eyelets. Use paper piercer to create holes and secure bookplate (see "Setting Eyelets" on p. 219).

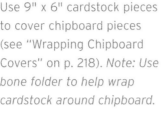

STEP FOUR
Center and adhere 6¾" x 3¾" cardstock to unfinished sides of covers.

STEP FIVE
Print title page on one 7" x 4" piece of cardstock.

STEP SIX
Stack filler pages between front and back covers and take to local office supply store for wire binding. *Note: Call ahead to your office supply store to ensure that they wire bind.*

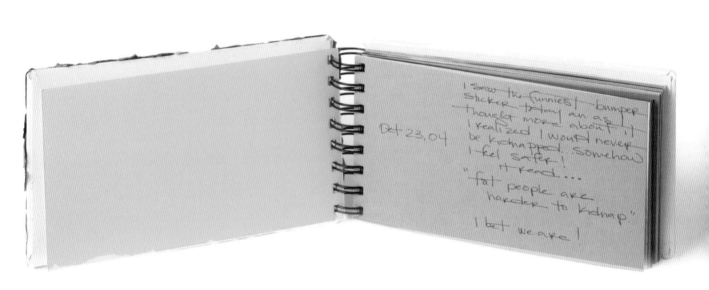

tell me a story

ALTERED BOARD BOOK

This may be my favorite project in the whole book, not because it's the most creative or best designed, but because it has the most sentimental meaning. In a nutshell, I'm constantly asking my husband to tell me a story. He hates this because he feels put on the spot. So I decided to make a storybook about us. After I explained my idea, he surprised me with several stories of his own to include in our storybook. I found this board book at my local dollar store, and it is the perfect base from which to construct a story book of our own.

SUPPLIES

- 6" x 6" board book
- 32 8½" x 11" pieces of cardstock
- clear stickers, sticker letters, and sticker tags
- crocheted flowers
- mini-brads
- two 6" x 6" pieces of patterned paper
- 6" length of bookbinding tape

TOOLS

- sanding block
- craft knife
- self-healing cutting mat
- paper trimmer
- scissors

ADHESIVE

- Xyron machine

MATERIALS

patterned paper, stickers, tags, crocheted flowers (SEI) • brads, bookbinding tape (Making Memories) • SansSerif font

Tell me a story...

While dating from several states away, Bill and I would share hour-long phone calls and often wrote long-winded letters to each other. However, when we graduated college and moved to North Carolina together, we no longer needed the phone calls and letters to keep in touch and that piece of the equation was lost. In a desperate attempt to recapture a little piece of that conversation back, I began asking my husband to "tell me a story"...in all honesty he may hate those four words more than any other words I utter. It puts him on the spot and he just clams up.

So I decided to make Bill a "story" book and shared with him the kinds of stories I treasured and wanted to include in it. A week later he surprised me...in an email he sent me several of his stories to be included in the book with a message that read, "All good stories have a happy ending."

altered board book step-by-step

STEP ONE
Print text for filler pages on cardstock, and trim to 6" x 6". Adhere to book pages. Use craft knife or sanding block to remove excess paper edges.

STEP TWO
Add embellishments to each page. *Note: If your book won't close after you've added card-stock and embellishments, try removing the original spine. You'll add a new one in Step 4.*

STEP THREE
Adhere patterned paper pieces to front and back covers. Use sanding block to remove excess paper edges. *Note: Patterned paper will not cover spine.*

STEP FOUR
Cover spine with bookbinding tape.

STEP FIVE
Print two title strips on cardstock, and trim each to 6" x ½". Adhere along tape edges, on both front and back covers.

Helpful Tip

I covered a children's board book, but you can order blank board books from:

blankslatebooks.com

ctpub.com

stampington.com

westrimcrafts.com

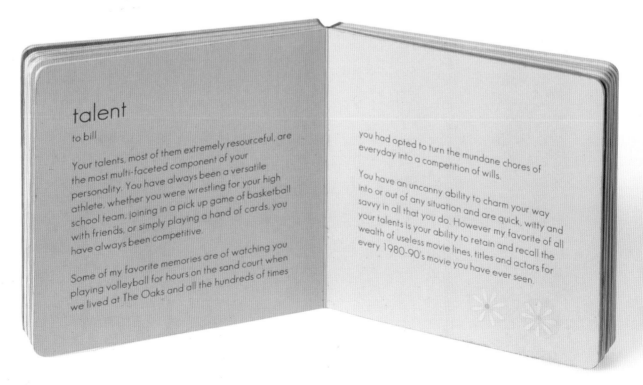

talent
to bill

Your talents, most of them extremely resourceful, are the most multi-faceted component of your personality. You have always been a versatile athlete, whether you were wrestling for your high school team, joining in a pick up game of basketball with friends, or simply playing a hand of cards, you have always been competitive.

Some of my favorite memories are of watching you playing volleyball for hours on the sand court when we lived at The Oaks and all the hundreds of times

you had opted to turn the mundane chores of everyday into a competition of wills.

You have an uncanny ability to charm your way into or out of any situation and are quick, witty and savvy in all that you do. However my favorite of all your talents is your ability to retain and recall the wealth of useless movie lines, titles and actors for every 1980-90's movie you have ever seen.

when one door closes

ENVELOPE ACCORDION JOURNAL

Totally inspired by the patterned paper, I created this envelope journal to house my collection of favorite quotes and what they mean to me. Filled with inspiration and personal insight, the journal is easy to update. As I have additional thoughts, I simply make more key tags and slip them in the envelopes.

envelope accordion journal step-by-step

STEP ONE
Use 11" x 6" patterned paper pieces to cover chipboard pieces (see "Wrapping Chipboard Covers" on p. 218).

STEP TWO
Print title on 8½" x 11" cardstock and trim to fit behind bookplate. Pierce guide holes for brads and attach to front cover.

STEP THREE
To create accordion spine, adhere back sides of 12" x 4" patterned paper pieces together.

STEP FOUR
Accordion-fold lengthwise every ⅝" until there are eight mountains. Trim off excess mountains.

STEP FIVE
Center and adhere top end of accordion to front cover and bottom end of accordion to back cover.

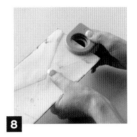

STEP SIX
Adhere 8¾" x 4¼" pieces of cardstock over inside covers to conceal wrapped edges.

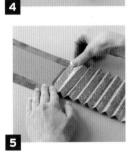

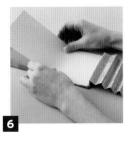

STEP SEVEN
Seal all envelopes and trim 1¼" from right edge of each. Print text directly on envelopes (see "Printing on Tags" on p. 220).

STEP EIGHT
Using circle punch, punch half circle from open edge of each envelope. *Note: Ink edges of envelopes for a weathered look.*

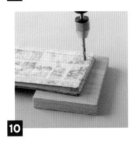

STEP NINE
Place one envelope in each valley. *Note: I used a little bit of adhesive to secure the envelopes.*

STEP TEN
Drill two holes through front cover, accordion spine, envelope pages, and back cover.

STEP ELEVEN
Thread twine through holes. Tie on front cover.

STEP TWELVE
Add text, stamped images, and embellishments to 8¼" x 4" cardstock pieces. Trim corners of each piece to create tag shape.

STEP THIRTEEN
Using handheld punch, create hole in top of tags. Attach vintage keys using large jump rings.

STEP FOURTEEN
Slip embellished cardstock pieces inside envelopes.

diZerega designs

BUSINESS JOURNAL

My neighbor, Heather diZerega, recently started her own business making handmade clothes. She showed me her Rubbermaid tub filled with patterns and an inexpensive photo album that she shows to prospective customers. Certainly I couldn't let her peddle her wares that way, so I created this fabric-covered journal. Inside, there are three sections, one each, for order forms and notes, scans of all her patterns, and pictures of her finished pieces.

SUPPLIES

- two 7¼" x 9¼" pieces of cardboard
- 1½" x 9¼" piece of cardboard
- 12" x 19" piece of upholstery fabric
- bookplate
- two flower brads
- 8½" x 11" piece of cardstock
- two 8" x 8½" pieces of self-adhesive fabric
- 9" length of bookbinding tape
- 25-30 7" x 9" sheets of copy paper and cardstock
- 2-3 plastic report covers
- two 18" lengths of ribbon

TOOLS

- pinking sheers or scissors
- paper trimmer
- paper piercer and push pad
- eyelet anywhere hole punch
- two-hole punch or handheld hole punch
- hammer

ADHESIVE

- all-purpose glue
- strips

MATERIALS

ribbon (Offray) • self-adhesive fabric (Shortcuts) • brads (Making Memories) • bookplate (*twopeasinabucket.com*) • Andale Mono font

business journal step-by-step

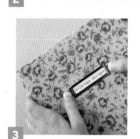

STEP ONE
Lay upholstery fabric flat, patterned side down. Center and adhere all three cardboard pieces on fabric, with smallest piece (spine) in center. Leave ¼" space between each piece.

STEP TWO
Let dry 5 min. Beginning with corners, wrap and adhere fabric around cardstock pieces (see "Wrapping Chipboard Covers" on p. 218).

STEP THREE
Print title on 8½" x 11" cardstock and trim to fit behind bookplate. Use paper piercer to punch guide holes through cover for brads. Attach bookplate.

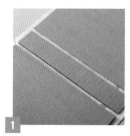

STEP FOUR
Adhere self-adhesive fabric to inside front and back covers, leaving a ½" border around outside edges. *Note: Fabric pieces should overlap in the middle, over spine.*

STEP FIVE
Adhere bookbinding tape to inside spine.

STEP SIX
Punch each 7" x 9" filler page with two-hole punch. *Note: You can also use a handheld hole punch.* To make dividers, trim report covers to 7¼" x 9¼" and punch with two-hole punch.

STEP SEVEN
Use one pre-punched filler page to mark placement of holes in covers. Use anywhere hole punch, with largest punch head, to puncture holes through covers. *Note: You may need to punch cover more than once.*

STEP EIGHT
Thread ribbons through album covers and pages, and tie in bows at spine (see "Tying a Bow" on p. 222). *Note: Be sure to leave some slack to allow journal to open.*

family expenses

CHECKBOOK COVER

How clever is this? You're sure to turn a few heads in line at the grocery store when you whip out a customized checkbook cover from your purse. The plastic covers are inexpensive and easy to decorate. I hope you haven't been throwing away those index prints that come with your photo orders, because they'll come in handy for this project.

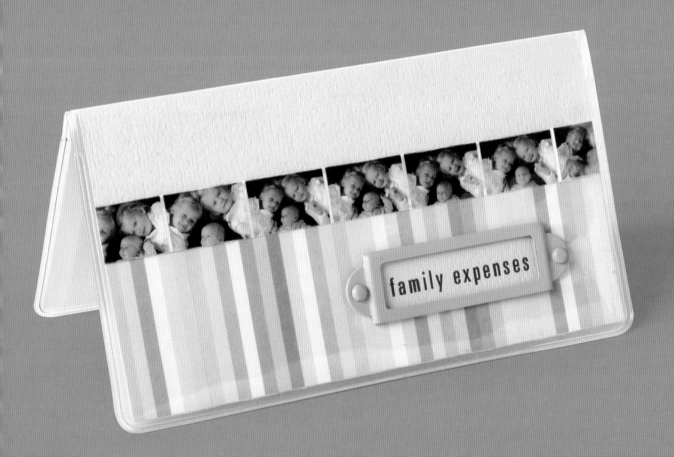

SUPPLIES

- clear checkbook cover
- two 5⅞" x 2" pieces of patterned paper
- 5⅞" x 6⅜" piece of cardstock
- photo index prints
- 8½" x 11" piece of cardstock
- bookplate
- two brads

TOOLS

- paper trimmer
- black pen
- paper piercer

ADHESIVE

- photo tabs

MATERIALS

checkbook cover (American Kelco Industries) • patterned paper (KI Memories) • bookplate, brads (Making Memories) • Univers Ultra Condensed font

checkbook cover step-by-step

1

2

3

4

5

STEP ONE
Adhere patterned paper across top and bottom of 5⅞" x 6⅜" cardstock.

STEP TWO
Fold in half so that patterned paper is on bottom of each folded side.

STEP THREE
Create two 5⅞" photo strips from index prints. Adhere strips over patterned paper edge on both front and back.

STEP FOUR
Print title on 8½" x 11" cardstock and trim to fit behind bookplate. Slide cardstock into plastic cover, then use black pen to mark hole placement on cover for brads.

STEP FIVE
Slide cardstock out of plastic cover. With hand in plastic cover pocket, use paper piercer to create guide holes for brads, and attach bookplate.

STEP SIX
Re-insert cardstock.

Project Variations

Using this same technique and a clear, checkbook-sized cover, customize a cover for the following:

- datebook
- calendar
- to-do list
- daily diet planner
- favorite recipes
- address book
- notepad

Purchase premade inserts for these items, or make your own using cardstock or copy paper. I bought my clear checkbook covers from *americankelco.com*.

Create your own slip-in covers and inserts for other clear items such as:

- business card holders
- menu covers
- book covers
- video or DVD cases

I covered a clear VHS case and made a small journal to fit inside. Look for this project in *Simple Scrapbooks'* special issue *Simple Inspirations*. For more details, visit *simplescrapbooksmag.com*.

too silly

SPIRAL NOTEBOOK JOURNAL

My kids really do say the darndest things. But I don't always have the time to stop and scrapbook all the laugh-out-loud moments of my life. So I came up with this 42-cent solution: a plain spiral-bound notebook transformed into a journal, documenting what I want to remember about my kids. I included the funny little things they say, wear, or simply do when they think I'm not looking.

SUPPLIES

- 6" x 9½" three-subject spiral notebook
- white spray paint
- 5½" x 9½" piece of patterned paper
- 40" length of ribbon
- letter stickers
- cardstock
- nine brads

TOOLS

- paper trimmer
- cardboard box
- portable die-cut machine
- 1¼" x ¾" rectangle index tab die

ADHESIVE

- Xyron machine
- strips

MATERIALS

patterned paper (Scrapworks) • ribbon (Textured Trios) • letter stickers (Li'l Davis Designs) • portable die-cut machine and index tab die (Sizzix) • Times font

spiral notebook journal step-by-step

STEP ONE
Hold book at 45° angle and spray light coat of paint along spine. Let dry and repeat for desired coverage. *Note: Make sure to turn pages between coats to ensure paint is not adhering spine to cover.*

STEP TWO
Adhere patterned paper to cover, leaving ½" of painted spine exposed.

STEP THREE
Run glue strip along edge where paper meets spine. Wrap ribbon around cover, over glue strip, and tie bow (see "Tying a Bow" on p. 222).

STEP FOUR
Adhere letter stickers to cover.

STEP FIVE
Print tab titles on cardstock. Die-cut three tabs from card-stock. Trim to fit inside tabs.

STEP SIX
Place tabs, in cascading positions, to right sides of notebook dividers, and secure with three brads per tab. *Note: If you don't have a portable die-cut machine, you can use office index tabs.*

phone numbers

My new favorite place to shop for interesting ideas is the dollar section at Super Target. Not that I didn't love Target before, but now I really can't stop myself from buying something because, well, it's only a dollar. This visit I found a purse-sized address book. I covered up the motif I wasn't too crazy about and added some index tabs. Hang on to your old address book. Like a journal, it's a simple way to remember friends, places, and acquaintances of years past.

SUPPLIES

- 3½" x 6¼" address book
- two 3" x 6" pieces of cardstock (color 1)
- two 3" x 4¼" pieces of cardstock (color 2)
- two 3" x ¼" pieces of cardstock (color 3)
- 8½" x 11" piece of cardstock (color 2)
- metal frame
- 8" length of ribbon
- alphabet tabs

TOOLS

- paper trimmer
- hammer
- push pad

ADHESIVE

- double-sided tape

alphabet tabs (Autumn Leaves) • metal frame (Scrapworks) • ribbon (May Arts) • Times New Roman font

address book journal step-by-step

STEP ONE
To create front and back covers, adhere 3" x 4¼" cardstock pieces to bottom portions of 3" x 6" cardstock pieces.

STEP TWO
Adhere 3" x ¼" cardstock pieces across seams.

STEP THREE
Adhere cardstock pieces to front and back of book.

STEP FOUR
Print title on 8½" x 11" cardstock and trim to fit behind frame.

STEP FIVE
Tie ribbon in bow around frame. Attach frame to front cover. Use hammer and push pad to press frame teeth into cover.

STEP SIX
Adhere alphabet tabs to filler pages.

Project Variations

Sometimes you *can* judge a book by its cover. Consider using the same technique for the following:

- Cover a recipe book with papers and embellishments
  to match your kitchen decor.

- Decorate an old school box or cigar box.

- Re-cover folders or notepads that have company or team logos.

in my prayers

BOOKMAKING KIT JOURNAL

Small enough to slip into a purse, this special journal is a place for recording my personal prayers and spiritual reflections. Even though you can make the book from scratch, I cheated and bought an inexpensive bookmaking kit and customized the cover with fabric and ribbon.

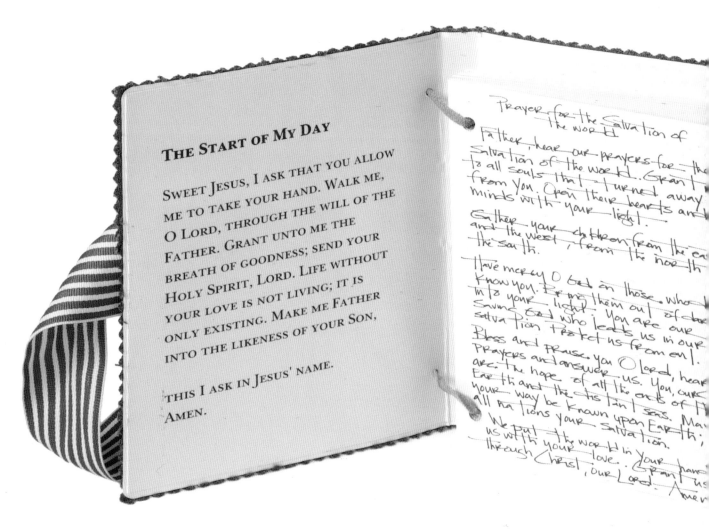

THE START OF MY DAY

SWEET JESUS, I ASK THAT YOU ALLOW ME TO TAKE YOUR HAND. WALK ME, O LORD, THROUGH THE WILL OF THE FATHER. GRANT UNTO ME THE BREATH OF GOODNESS; SEND YOUR HOLY SPIRIT, LORD. LIFE WITHOUT YOUR LOVE IS NOT LIVING; IT IS ONLY EXISTING. MAKE ME FATHER INTO THE LIKENESS OF YOUR SON,

THIS I ASK IN JESUS' NAME. AMEN.

bookmaking kit journal step-by-step

STEP ONE

Wrap and adhere one piece of fabric, trimmed to 12" x 3", around top of book cover. *Note: Do not wrap fabric around the cover edges.*

STEP TWO

Repeat Step 1, trimming second piece of fabric to 12" x 4". Wrap fabric around bottom of book, slightly overlapping first piece of fabric.

STEP THREE

Apply thin line of repositionable adhesive where two fabrics meet. Wrap ribbon around book, over seam, leaving two long, loose ends.

STEP FOUR

Zig-zag stitch ribbon to cover along top, bottom, and sides.

STEP FIVE

Print title on 8½" x 11" cardstock and trim to fit behind bookplate. Use paper piercer to punch guide holes for brads. Attach to cover, over ribbon, with mini-brads.

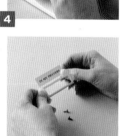

STEP SIX

Adhere 11¾" x 6¾" cardstock over inside cover to conceal stitches and brads. *Note: I printed a prayer on the cardstock before adhering it to the cover.*

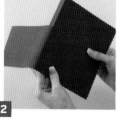

STEP SEVEN

Use kit template to mark top and bottom hole placement on book pages. Punch holes in pages, using handheld punch.

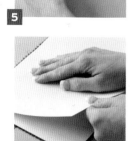

STEP EIGHT

Punch top and bottom holes in cover, using anywhere hole punch.

STEP NINE

To bind pages and cover, thread leather cording through holes.

Helpful Tip

Make your own book with supplies you have on hand. For the cover, trim cardstock or chipboard to 11¾" x 7". To create spine, score and fold widthwise at 5⁹⁄₁₆" and 6⁵⁄₁₆". Trim pieces of cardstock for pages, punch holes, and bind.

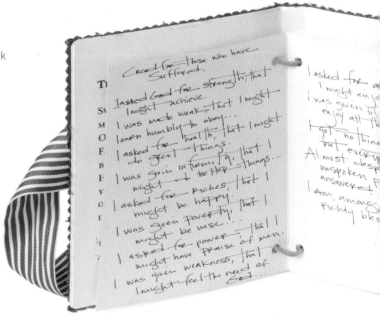

a little gratitude

TIE-THROUGH JOURNAL

Sometimes it's nice to just stop and smell the roses and write down the things that you're most grateful for. It may be a moment, a photo, or a great sale. Use a gratitude journal to document the things that make you smile. Before you know it you'll have assembled an entire scrapbook documenting the extraordinary in the ordinary. I sure wish my grandmother had left one of these for me!

SUPPLIES

- 4" x 5½" hardbound journal
- 9" x 5¾" piece of patterned paper
- two 5⅛" x 7¼" pieces of cardstock
- acrylic paint
- cardstock
- bookplate

- two brads
- two eyelets
- 18" length of thin ribbon

TOOLS

- paper trimmer
- sanding block
- foam brush
- hand drill and largest bit
- eyelet-setting tools
- paper piercer
- push pad
- hand clamp (optional)

ADHESIVE

- Xyron machine or decoupage adhesive
- photo tabs

MATERIALS

patterned paper (Paper Adventures) • bookplate, snaps, eyelets, acrylic paint (Making Memories) • ribbon (May Arts) • hand drill (Fiskars) • Bernhard Modern and P22 Cezanne Regular fonts

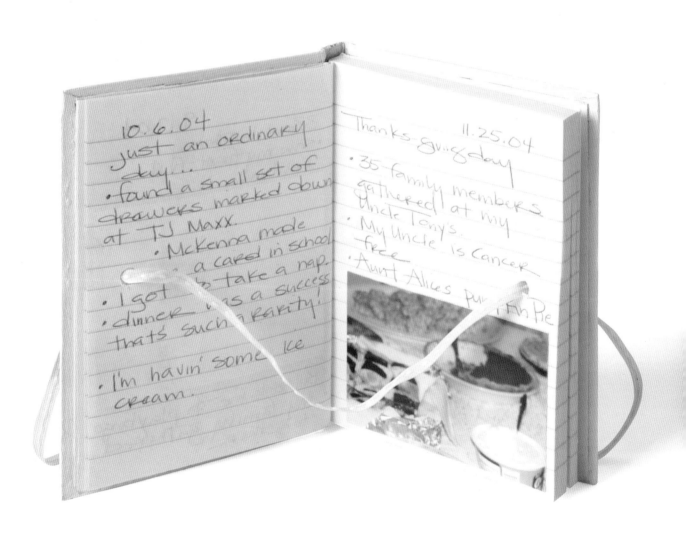

tie-through journal step-by-step

STEP ONE
Apply adhesive to back of patterned paper. Adhere to journal, starting with front cover, and wrapping around to back. Use sanding block to remove any excess paper (see "Sanding" on p. 221).

STEP TWO
Brush thin coat of acrylic paint to exposed edges of both front and back covers and spine. Let dry. If necessary, apply another coat. *Note: It's okay to be sloppy with the paint!*

STEP THREE
Print title on cardstock and trim to fit behind bookplate. Use paper piercer to create guide holes for brads and attach bookplate to front cover.

STEP FOUR
Fold 5⅛" x 7¼" cardstock in half lengthwise. Adhere to inside front cover and first page. Repeat for inside back cover and last page.

STEP FIVE
Drill hole for ribbon ½" from journal edge, through covers and all pages. *Note: Have someone hold the journal in place while drilling, or use a hand clamp.*

STEP SIX
Set eyelets through hole in front and back cover, making sure finished sides of eyelets are on outside (see "Setting Eyelets" on p. 219).

STEP SEVEN
Thread ribbon through covers and pages. Tie in bow.

Helpful Tip

Believe it or not, the original hardbound journal I used is actually a Winnie the Pooh notebook I bought at a dollar store. Be sure to use heavier patterned paper or cardstock to decorate books that have bright images on their covers. Lighter patterned paper may not conceal the images.

i want to be a size 12

INDEX CARD JOURNAL

Keeping a weight-loss journal is just one step to a healthier lifestyle. Now that I've publicly announced my intentions, I feel a bit liberated. When I reach my size 12 goal, I can remove the perforated journaling cards and add them to my size 12 scrapbook. Well, I'm off to the gym. Wish me luck!

SUPPLIES

- 6" x 4" perforated index card notebook
- two colors of acrylic paint
- 6" x 1¼" piece of patterned paper
- 6" x 3" piece of patterned paper
- 18" length of printed twill ribbon
- stencil numbers
- ribbon charm letters

TOOLS

- paper trimmer
- small paintbrush
- foam brushes

ADHESIVE

- Xyron machine
- dot adhesive sheet

MATERIALS

patterned paper (Chatterbox, KI Memories) • printed twill (Carolee's Creations) • acrylic paint, stencil letters, ribbon charm letters (Making Memories)

index card journal step-by-step

STEP ONE
Using small paintbrush, paint notebook cover between rings at spine. Repeat coats if necessary. Let dry completely.

STEP TWO
Adhere 6" x 1¼" patterned paper next to spine.

STEP THREE
Adhere 6" x 3" patterned paper to rest of cover, slightly overlapping first paper.

STEP FOUR
To conceal paper seam, wrap twill ribbon around cover and tie in knot.

STEP FIVE
Paint stencil numbers with second color of acrylic paint. Let dry.

STEP SIX
Embellish cover by adhering stencil numbers and metal letters.

Project Variations

This index card concept can work for all sorts of journal topics. Pick a topic and keep your journal handy. Then when you scrapbook, tear out a card and use it for journaling. Here are a few ideas:

- Create a book of your favorite quotes or advice.

- Write on one card every week or every month to record your feelings about a new spouse, a new child, or the friends who make your life interesting.

- Record your thoughts and challenges as you tackle a new goal. Whether you're trying to exercise more, reduce personal debt, find a new job, improve a relationship, or buy a new car, documenting your progress can help you achieve your goals.

flower garden

BEADED CHAIN JOURNAL

Traditionally, my husband is the one with the green thumb. But this year I decided to take a stab at flower gardening around the house. In preparation, I created a garden journal to track important information about the blooms, including their placement, sun and water requirements, and their progress throughout the season. Now each spring I can look back at my journal and better understand just how my garden grows.

SUPPLIES
- 8" round journal
- 12" x 12" piece of textured paper
- 12" x 12" piece of patterned paper
- three large silk flowers
- 12" x 12" transparency
- three decorative brads
- wooden letters
- ribbon charm letters

TOOLS
- craft knife
- self-healing cutting mat
- paper piercer
- handheld hole punch

ADHESIVE
- dot adhesive sheet
- Xyron machine

MATERIALS
round journal (DMD, Inc.) • textured paper (Provo Craft) • patterned paper (Chatterbox) • transparency (Creative Imaginations) • wood letters (Li'l Davis Designs) • ribbon charm letters, decorative brads (Making Memories)

beaded chain journal step-by-step

STEP ONE
Remove journal cover from chain binding.

STEP TWO
Place textured paper face down. Apply adhesive to front cover of journal and adhere to paper. Use craft knife to trim away excess paper. Use hand punch to repunch hole through cover.

STEP THREE
Remove stems and centers from flowers. Position flowers and title on cover. Use paper piercer to punch guide holes through cover, and attach flowers with decorative brads.

STEP FOUR
Use dot adhesive sheet to adhere title letters to cover. *Note: Place back of letter on adhesive sheet and lift.*

STEP FIVE
Place patterned paper face down. Apply adhesive to back of front cover and adhere to paper. Use craft knife to trim away paper. Repunch hole.

STEP SIX
Remove back cover from chain. Use cover as template to cut transparency to size. Adhere cover to transparency, using one photo tab. Trim away excess transparency, and punch hole through transparency for binding. Remove transparency and place between front cover and first page of journal.

STEP SEVEN
Replace back cover. Rethread chain through front cover, transparency, filler pages, and back cover.

inspired house

HOME DECOR JOURNAL

My friend Karen is a savvy decorator. Her home has some of the most amazing combinations of color and stylistic touches. She used to keep a traveling designer's folder stashed in the trunk of her car to use as a reference when shopping, in which she loosely stored various magazine clippings, fabric swatches, and notes. Inspired by her folder, I personalized for her a spiral-bound journal with a new cover, and made tabs and sections for each room of her home. Now Karen compiles her home decor ideas in one bound, portable journal to take on her shopping excursions.

SUPPLIES

- 9" x 11" spiral-bound journal
- home decor magazine cover
- 8½" x 11" piece of photo paper
- five bookplates
- 30 mini-brads
- cardstock
- 40-50 3" lengths of ribbon

ADHESIVE

- Xyron machine
- photo tabs

MATERIALS

spiral-bound sketch book (DMD, Inc.) • ribbon (Paper House Productions, Textured Trios) • bookplates, brads (Making Memories) • magazine cover (*Inspired House magazine*) • portable die-cut machine and index tab die (Sizzix) • Helvetica Neue font

TOOLS

- paper trimmer
- handheld hole punch
- scissors
- paper piercer and push pad
- portable die-cut machine
- 2⅛" x 1½" triangle index tab die
- 2½" circle punch

STEP ONE

Slightly bend apart spiral binding of journal to remove cover.

STEP TWO

Adhere magazine cover to journal cover. Repunch holes through cover for spiral binding. Reassemble book.

STEP THREE

Print five subtitles on photo paper, and trim to fit behind bookplates (see "Printing Reverse Text" on p. 220). Attach bookplates to cover, using paper piercer to create guide holes for brads.

STEP FOUR

Die-cut six tabs from cardstock. Print tab titles on cardstock and trim to fit inside tabs. *Note: If you don't have a die-cut machine, you can use office index tabs.*

STEP FIVE

Place tabs, in cascading positions, to right sides of journal pages and secure with three brads per tab.

STEP SIX

Tie assorted ribbon around spine. Using circle punch, punch photo and add to cover.

Project Variations

So what if you're not a savvy decorator? Use this project format to scrapbook each room of your home. Take pictures of your favorite places to read, relax, or entertain. In twenty years, you can look back and chuckle at the out-of-style colors and decor. Try using different magazine covers for themed journals:

- *Newsweek*—Make a section for each month and document newsworthy events and accomplishments.
- *Child*—Assign each child in your family a section.
- *People*—Divide the journal into seasons or events. Take pictures of your best-dressed moments.

to do

PRONG FASTENER JOURNAL

This is no ordinary to-do list, but rather a documentation of a day in my life. Create an attractive purse-sized journal to keep your daily tasks organized and accessible. Use the inside clip to attach essential reminders you may need to turn your "to-do's" into "done."

SUPPLIES

- 10" x 12" piece of patterned paper
- 1" x 8" piece of chipboard
- two 5" x 8" pieces of chipboard
- 7¾" x 10¾" piece of cardstock
- 1¼" x 2¾" piece of cardstock
- 40 4¾" x 7½" pieces of card-stock or copy paper
- prong fastener
- letter stickers
- wooden frame
- bulldog clip

TOOLS

- paper trimmer
- bone folder
- pencil
- handheld hole punch or two-hole punch

ADHESIVE

- Xyron machine
- strips

MATERIALS

patterned paper, letter stickers (K&Company) • wooden frame (Li'l Davis Designs) • prong fastener

prong fastener journal step-by-step

STEP ONE
Lay patterned paper face down. Center and adhere 1" x 8" chipboard.

STEP TWO
Adhere 5" x 8" pieces of chipboard on either side of first chipboard, leaving ¼" spaces in between.

STEP THREE
Treat chipboard pieces as one large, continuous piece, and place glue strips around outside edge. Wrap patterned paper around chipboard (see "Wrapping Chipboard Covers" on p. 218).

STEP FOUR
Center and adhere 7¾" x 10¾" cardstock to entire inside cover, covering unfinished edges.

STEP FIVE
Score and fold paper where chipboard pieces meet to create front, spine, and back.

STEP SIX
Mark placement of holes, and punch holes in cardstock or copy paper using two-hole punch or hand punch. *Note: Use one punched cardstock page as a guide to mark placement of holes on back inside cover. Punch holes through cover.*

STEP SEVEN
Insert fastener into holes. Fasten filler pages to journal.

STEP EIGHT
Center and adhere letter stickers to 1½" x 2¾" piece of cardstock. Attach cardstock behind wooden frame, and adhere frame to cover.

STEP NINE
Add bulldog clip to top of front cover.

a mother's journal

COMPOSITION JOURNAL

Some of the best, most memorable, empowering, tiresome, emotional, and maybe even worst days of a new mother's journey are during the first few years of her child's life. Without the constraints of traditional scrapbooking, this sweet journal is an accessible place to record these moments and a mother's thoughts throughout the day. Personalize it with a photo and it makes a great gift.

SUPPLIES

- 7½" x 9¾" composition notebook
- two 7" x 10" pieces of cardstock
- 10" length of bookbinding tape
- three 2½" x 6" pieces of patterned paper
- two 8½" x 11" pieces of cardstock
- two bookplates
- four brads
- letter stickers
- three 2" x 1½" pieces of patterned paper
- 36" length of ribbon
- stamp pad

TOOLS

- paper trimmer
- craft knife
- self-healing cutting mat
- sanding block
- scissors

ADHESIVE

- Xyron machine
- photo tabs

MATERIALS

patterned paper, bookplates, ribbon, bookbinding tape (Making Memories) • letter stickers (SEI) • stamp pad (Ranger Industries) • Times New Roman font

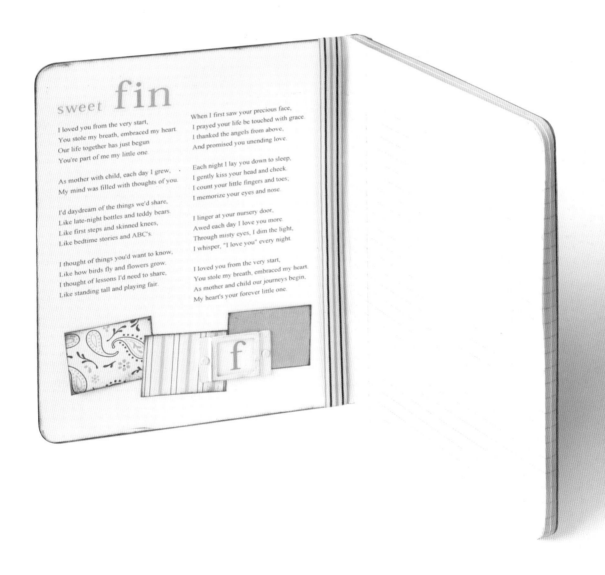

composition journal step-by-step

STEP ONE
Adhere 7" x 10" cardstock pieces to front and back covers, making sure to leave part of spine exposed.

STEP TWO
Use craft knife to trim excess paper edges, and smooth edges, using sanding block (see "Sanding" on p. 221).

STEP THREE
Wrap bookbinding tape around spine.

STEP FOUR
Gently rub stamp pad across both cover edges and 2½" x 6" patterned paper edges. *Note: This technique is called "inking" and adds a weathered, vintage look to the project.* Overlap and adhere patterned paper pieces to front cover.

STEP FIVE
Use sanding block to weather edges of photo, then adhere photo over patterned paper.

STEP SIX
Print subtitle on 8½" x 11" cardstock and trim to fit behind bookplate. Use paper piercer to punch guide holes through and attach bookplate with brads (see "Piercing Guide Holes" on p. 221).

STEP SEVEN
Add sticker title.

STEP EIGHT
For inside cover, print journaling on 8½" x 11" cardstock. *Note: I used a poem found on two-peasinabucket.com.* Ink edges of 2" x 1½" patterned papers, and adhere to printed card-stock. Embellish cardstock with stickers and bookplate.

STEP NINE
Adhere cardstock to inside front cover. Use craft knife to trim excess paper edges, and sanding block to smooth edges. Ink edges of cardstock.

STEP TEN
Wrap ribbon around front cover, near spine, and tie in bow (see "Tying a Bow" on p. 222).

to do, to go, to see

DATEBOOK JOURNAL

Since I use my datebook practically every day, I wanted it to be accessible but also a reflection of my personality. And since I'm not a brown planner kinda gal, I used my favorite colors and designs instead. I even sprinkled a few brightly colored paint chips and string envelopes between the calendar pages. There's plenty of room for my notes, receipts, and photos. It's got "me" written all over it!

SUPPLIES
- 52 12" x 6" pieces of cardstock
- two 11¾" x 8¼" pieces of patterned paper
- two 9¾" x 6¼" pieces of chipboard
- 8½" x 11" piece of cardstock
- bookplate and four eyelets
- two 9½" x 5¾" pieces of cardstock
- 8" length of ribbon
- assorted paint chips and string envelopes

TOOLS
- paper trimmer
- eyelet-setting tools

ADHESIVE
- Xyron machine

MATERIALS
patterned paper (KI Memories) • bookplate (Li'l Davis Designs) • string envelopes (Waste Not Paper) • ribbon (Offray) • Adler font

datebook journal step-by-step

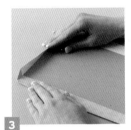

STEP ONE
Print weekly calendar on 12" x 6" cardstock pieces. *Note: Change document orientation to landscape (horizontal). I inserted a table with 7 columns and 2 rows to create my weekly calendar. Make sure the table isn't larger than 8½" x 5½".*

STEP TWO
Trim pages to 9½" x 6".

STEP THREE
Use patterned paper to wrap chipboard pieces (see "Wrapping Chipboard Covers" p. 218).

STEP FOUR
Print journal title on 8½" x 11" cardstock, and trim to fit behind bookplate. Wrap ribbon around bookplate, and attach bookplate to front cover with eyelets (see "Setting Eyelets" p. 219).

STEP FIVE
Print quotes or journaling on 9½" x 5¾" cardstock pieces, and center and adhere to inside front and back covers.

STEP SIX
Place paint chips and envelopes between journal pages. *Note: Make sure to distribute items along the top, middle, and bottom. Attaching them all in the same spot may make the journal uneven.*

STEP SEVEN
Stack filler pages, envelopes, and paint chips between covers and take to office supply or copy store for wire binding. *Note: Call ahead to ensure that they wire bind.*

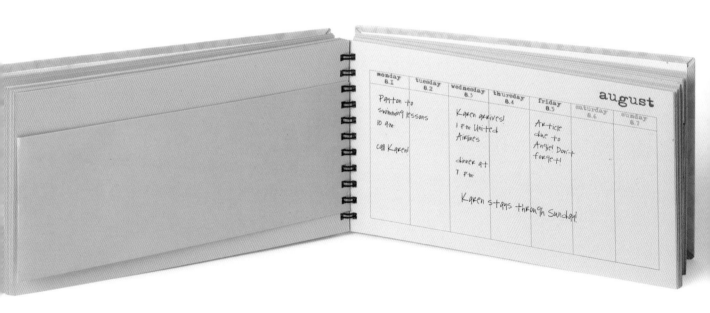

travel log

DOUBLE SPINE JOURNAL

This unconventional take on a traditional travel journal is like two journals in one: use the large journal for capturing your thoughts as you visit and experience different sites, and use the small journal for the who-what-when-where-and-why details of your trip. There's even a section for photos and memorabilia collected along the way. This is a journal I can't wait to complete someday. Anyone wanna baby-sit?

SUPPLIES

- 19" x 27" piece of patterned paper
- 12" x 8" piece of chipboard
- 11¾" x 7¾" piece of cardstock
- 8" x 8" piece of chipboard
- 7¾" x 7¾" piece of cardstock
- 8½" x 11" piece of cardstock
- 3" x 8" piece of chipboard
- 2¾" x 7¾" piece of cardstock
- 25-50 12" x 12" pieces of cardstock
- cardstock
- three eyelets

TOOLS

- paper trimmer
- bone folder
- portable die-cut machine
- 2⅛" x 1½" triangle index tab die
- eyelet-setting tools

ADHESIVE

- Xyron machine

MATERIALS

patterned paper (Tassotti) • Confidential font • portable die-cut machine and index tab die (Sizzix)

double spine journal step-by-step

STEP ONE
To make base, trim 14" x 10" section from patterned paper and cover 12" x 8" chipboard (see "Wrapping Chipboard Covers" p. 218).

STEP TWO
Center and adhere 11¾" x 7¾" cardstock to unfinished side.

STEP THREE
To make larger front cover, trim 10" x 10" section from patterned paper and cover 8" x 8" chipboard. Center and adhere 7¾" x 7¾" cardstock to unfinished side.

STEP FOUR
Print title on 8½" x 11" cardstock (see "Printing Reverse Text" on p. 220) and trim to 5" x 10". Cover 3" x 8" chipboard. *Note: Use bone folder to help wrap cardstock around chipboard.*

STEP FIVE
Center and adhere 2¾" x 7¾ cardstock to unfinished side.

STEP SIX
Trim 8" x 8" filler pages from 12" x 12" cardstock. Use remaining paper scraps to trim same number of 3" x 8" filler pages.

STEP SEVEN
Die-cut one tab from cardstock. Print tab title in reverse text on cardstock and trim to fit inside tab. Place tab on top of cardstock piece, and secure with three eyelets (see "Setting Eyelets" p. 219). *Note: If you don't have a die-cut machine, you can use an office index tab.*

STEP EIGHT
Stack filler pages between covers and take to office supply or copy store for wire binding. *Note: Call ahead to ensure that they wire bind.*

Helpful Tip
I ordered the large sheet of patterned paper from an online site, *greatstuff4you.com*. Check your local art supply store or craft chain store for similar items, or search the Web for oversized sheets of patterned paper.

random advice

FILE BOX DIVIDER JOURNAL

I started keeping this random advice journal for my girls. It's a compilation of thoughts, ideas, quotes, and feelings organized into sections. I like to think of it as my "What would Mom say?" solution to issues my girls may face as they mature. As I have advice, I write it on a Post-it and stick it in the appropriate section. Once I've accumulated enough notes, I type them up.

SUPPLIES

- eight 6" x 6" pieces of patterned paper
- seven 4" x 6" file box dividers
- rub-on words and letters
- six ¾" x 2¼" pieces of cardstock
- six ⅜" x 6" pieces of cardstock
- six 4" x 6" photos
- six 4" x 6" pieces of cardstock
- acrylic paint
- two 1¼" binder rings
- seven 6" lengths of assorted ribbon
- cardstock
- vintage pocket watch case
- large jump ring or wire ring

TOOLS

- paper trimmer
- sanding block
- handheld or anywhere hole punch
- foam brush
- paper piercer and push pad
- brayer

ADHESIVE

- decoupage adhesive
- Xyron machine

MATERIALS

patterned paper, metal mailbox letter (Making Memories) • rub-ons (Making Memories, Chartpak) • ribbon (May Arts, Offray) • pocket watch case (eBay.com) • Gill Sans font

the random things I have learned

I believe maturity is a milestone you should never fully reach. Now I do not mean you can never behave maturely, however, every new day brings with it the hope of new opportunities and the chance for new experiences. Making a conscious choice to grow and learn more about yourself and your limitations is the greatest gift you can give yourself.

Many of the life lessons I have learned have been through either: trial and error, accident or just plain old luck. I have always been one to push the envelope or challenge the masses just to see if a situation had more to offer than what face value presented. Having said this, I have also learned that if your going to challenge anything you need to also be prepared for what the answers and outcome might be in the end. If you believe in something with conviction, no matter what the outcome it is worth the perserverance.

file box divider journal step-by-step

STEP ONE

Apply decoupage adhesive to front sides of dividers. Adhere 6" x 6" patterned paper. Use brayer to smooth out any air bubbles. Let dry 5 min. To make back cover, use remaining paper piece to cover back side of one divider.

STEP TWO

Use sanding block to remove excess paper (see "Sanding" on p. 221).

STEP THREE

Add rub-on title to cover, then add rub-on subtitles to divider tabs.

STEP FOUR

Adhere ¾" x 2¼" cardstock to back side of each uncovered tab. Use sanding block to remove excess paper.

STEP FIVE

Adhere 4" x 6" photos to back side of each uncovered divider. Sand edges of photo. Adhere ⅜" x 6" strips of cardstock along photo edge and underneath divider tab. Add rub-ons to photos.

STEP SIX

Print or write journaling on 4" x 6" cardstock. Brush acrylic paint on edges; let dry. Place behind dividers.

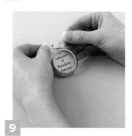

STEP SEVEN

Mark hole placement and punch holes for binder rings. Bind journal with rings.

STEP EIGHT

Tie assorted ribbon on binder rings.

STEP NINE

Print text on cardstock and trim to fit inside pocket watch. Embellish with ribbon.

STEP TEN

Use paper piercer to create guide hole in cover divider, and attach pocket watch using large jump ring.

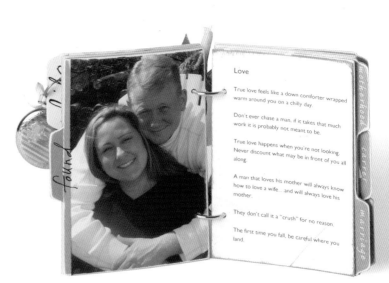

family game night

ELASTIC CLOSURE JOURNAL

I can totally hear my friend Karen saying, "Oh no, she did *not* make a Scrabble journal. She doesn't play Scrabble." That's completely true, and the only reason I don't play is because I *absolutely* stink at the game and *always* lose miserably. However, I do support those who enjoy the game. I made this journal for my friend Kris Parkin, who plays rather competitively with her son Troy.

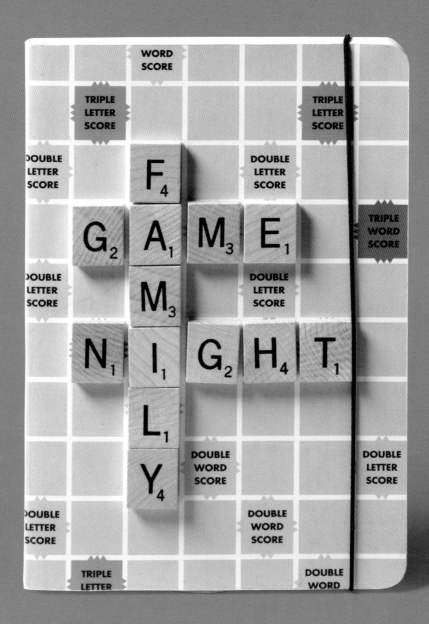

SUPPLIES

- 5¼" x 7¼" elastic band closure journal
- 7¾" x 12" piece of patterned paper
- Scrabble game pieces
- 10" elastic cord with metal stops

TOOLS

- paper trimmer
- craft knife
- self-healing cutting mat
- ⅛" hole punch

ADHESIVE

- Xyron machine
- dots

MATERIALS

patterned paper, Scrabble game pieces (EK Success) • elastic (7gypsies)

elastic closure journal step-by-step

STEP ONE
Remove original elastic from journal. *Note: You don't have to have an elastic closure journal.*

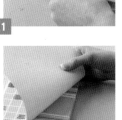

STEP TWO
Apply adhesive to back of paper. Adhere, starting with front cover, and wrapping around back.

STEP THREE
Trim away excess paper edges, using craft knife and cutting mat.

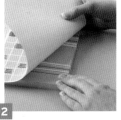

STEP FOUR
Adhere Scrabble game pieces to cover with adhesive dots. Spell out journal title.

STEP FIVE
Find covered holes in back cover with finger. Mark placement and re-punch two holes for elastic. *Note: If your original journal doesn't have elastic closure holes, punch holes approximately ¾" from side, and 2" from top and bottom.*

STEP SIX
Thread new elastic through holes and wrap around front of journal.

my inspiration

HANDMADE BINDER JOURNAL

My inspiration journal sits on my desk as a quick reference and perpetual source of inspiration. Divided into three tabbed sections, the journal documents my interests and the stylistic changes I have gone through as a scrapbook designer. It also provides basic steps for replicating projects as well as project variations.

SUPPLIES

- two 12" x 8" pieces of patterned paper
- 2½" x 5¾" piece of chipboard
- two 9½" x 5¾" pieces of chipboard
- two 11" x 5½" pieces of cardstock
- ¼" x 8" piece of cardstock
- two-ring binder spine
- 50-75 5½" x 8" pieces of copy paper
- nine eyelets and two extra-long eyelets
- three 8¼" x 5¾" pieces of chipboard
- six 8¼" x 5¾" pieces of patterned paper
- cardstock
- monogram sticker
- rub-on letters

TOOLS

- eyelet-setting tools
- paper trimmer
- pencil
- handheld hole punch
- portable die-cut machine
- 2⅛" x 1½" triangle index tab die
- bone folder

ADHESIVE

- Xyron machine
- photo tabs
- double-sided tape

MATERIALS

• patterned paper (Chatterbox) • eyelets, extra-long eyelets (Making Memories) • rub-ons (Autumn Leaves) • monogram sticker (My Mind's Eye)

handmade binder journal step-by-step

STEP ONE
Place two 12" x 8" patterned papers face down, side by side, so that they make one continuous sheet of 24" x 8" paper. Center and adhere 2½" x 5¾" chipboard over seam.

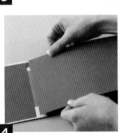

STEP TWO
Adhere 9½" x 5¾" chipboards on either side of first chipboard, leaving ¼" spaces in between.

STEP THREE
Treat chipboard pieces as one large, continuous piece, and apply double-sided tape around entire perimeter. Wrap patterned paper around chipboard. Start with corners, then fold in all sides (see "Wrapping Chipboard Covers" on p. 218).

STEP FOUR
Center and adhere 11" x 5½" cardstock pieces to unfinished cover, starting at center seam and adhering out.

STEP FIVE
Fold cover where chipboard pieces meet to create a front, spine, and back.

STEP SIX
To conceal seam on outside of spine, adhere ¼" x 8" cardstock over seam. Wrap ends around spine and fold over inside covers.

STEP SEVEN
Center binder on inside spine and mark placement for holes. Use anywhere hole punch and hammer to punch holes through spine. Attach binder to spine using extra-long eyelets (see "Setting Eyelets" on p. 219).

STEP EIGHT
Adhere 8¼" x 5¾" patterned paper to same size chipboard pieces, on both front and back. Sand paper edges for a weathered look (see "Sanding" on p. 221).

STEP NINE
Die-cut three tabs from cardstock. Print tab titles on cardstock and trim to fit inside tabs. Place tabs, in cascading positions, to sides of chipboard dividers and secure with three eyelets per tab. *Note: If you don't have a die-cut machine, you can use office index tabs.*

STEP TEN
Create a template for punching holes. Using template as guide, hand punch holes through pages and dividers. Add all section and filler pages.

STEP ELEVEN
Embellish cover with monogram sticker and rub-on letters.

tools and supplies

FLIP FRAME JOURNAL

I've been a little overwhelmed by my mounting scrapbooking supplies, so when I saw this photo flip frame I knew I had the perfect solution. I organized samples of my supplies—such as rubber stamp images, punches, stamp pad colors, etc.—in the pages of the book, so while I'm working I can quickly flip through an inventory of my tools and supplies without the distraction of searching my workspace.

SUPPLIES

- photo flip frame
- 6" x 4½" piece of cardstock
- seven 6½" x 4¼" pieces of cardstock
- rub-on letters
- 30-60 6" x 4¼" pieces of cardstock

TOOLS

- paper trimmer
- handheld hole punch
- scissors

ADHESIVE

- photo tabs
- dots

MATERIALS

photo flip frame (Target) • rub-on letters (Autumn Leaves) • Gill Sans font

flip frame journal step-by-step

STEP ONE

Print title on 6" x 4½" cardstock. Punch two holes in top of the cardstock to accommodate album rings.

STEP TWO

Remove first photo sleeve from frame and insert cardstock. Reassemble frame. *Note: Flower embellishments are already part of the frame.*

STEP THREE

Use one 6½" x 4¼" piece of cardstock to create divider template. Trace template on remaining 6½" x 4¼" cardstock pieces and trim to create dividers.

STEP FOUR

Add rub-ons to tabs, and slide dividers into sleeves.

STEP FIVE

Add information to 6½" x 4¼" cardstock pieces, and place in sleeves behind appropriate dividers.

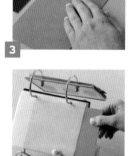

Project Variation

Decorate a flip frame to keep an inventory of items such as:

- colors and fabric patterns in your home
- sizes and types of clothing and shoes for yourself and family members
- CDs or DVDs
- favorite recipes
- wish lists for you and your loved ones

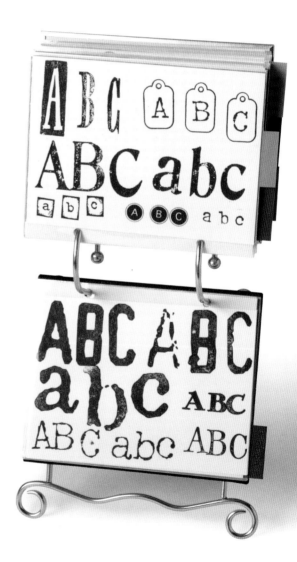

photo decor

simply love

UNFINISHED WOOD FRAMES

Sometimes I wonder if the paper fairy visits my home before she makes her next batch of coordinated patterned papers—because I can always find papers to match the color scheme of my decor. These small paper-covered frames create an eye-catching collage running across the stark white walls of my daughters' bedroom. Use the frames to highlight special traits of different family members or to share family stories.

be true TO YOU

authentic self

Your uniquely amazing ability to personify happiness with your every action is truly your gift. You live in the moment and fully immerse yourself in it at will, by celebrating with your own song and dance. You're an amazing little girl and I hope you always remain "true to you."

SIMPLY

love

Imagine...create

With an amazing ability to turn your ideas into tangible play, there is no doubt that you can achieve anything you put your mind to. Your initiative and determination sets you apart. Continue to push the envelope and challenge yourself; never loose your sense of wonder and "always dream."

SUPPLIES
- five 5" x 5" unfinished wood frames
- five 6" x 6" pieces of patterned paper
- rub-on words
- three 3¼" x 3¼" photos
- cardstock
- acrylic paint

TOOLS
- sanding block
- emery board or nail file
- paper trimmer
- two foam brushes
- brayer
- craft knife
- self-healing cutting mat

ADHESIVE
- decoupage adhesive

MATERIALS
unfinished wood frames (Provo Craft) • patterned paper, acrylic paint (Making Memories) • rub-ons (C-Thru Ruler Company) • Times New Roman, Marker Felt, and Donna Downey fonts

unfinished wood frames step-by-step

STEP ONE
Apply even coat of adhesive to each frame front, using foam brush. Adhere patterned paper. Roll brayer over surface of frame to smooth out any air bubbles. Let dry 2-3 min.

STEP TWO
Sand away excess edges of patterned paper, using sanding block.

STEP THREE
Lay frame flat, covered side down. Use craft knife to cut away paper from window. Sand away paper and smooth window edges with emery board.

STEP FOUR
Brush paint around outside edges and inside windows of frames. *Note: Don't worry about getting the paint on the patterned paper. A little sloppy painting gives the frame a shabby chic appeal.*

STEP FIVE
Write or print journaling on cardstock. Trim photos and journaling to fit behind windows (approx. ¼" larger than opening on all sides) and secure.

STEP SIX
Apply rub-on words to frames. Arrange on wall.

Helpful Tip

I wanted to add a personal touch to these frames, so I had my handwriting made into a true type font. I scanned and e-mailed a sample of my writing to *fontifier.com*, and they sent it back to me as a downloadable font for my computer.

p-l-a-y time

OVERSIZED WOODEN LETTERS

I'm a sucker for anything word-related—rubber stamps, rub-ons, printed twill ribbon, patterned papers, wooden letters. If it involves words, I've gotta have it. That's why I had to place these large wooden letters in my son Cole's room. Just cover them with your favorite patterned paper and use photos to embellish. Spell out any word you want and you've made w-o-n-d-e-r-f-u-l word decor.

With plenty of giggles, wide smiles and spontaneous squeals of jubilation. . . we PLAY.

time

Happy, energetic, curious, contented, playful and daring ...all encapsulated in one tiny body. You live every moment at play and are the most absolutely irresistible little boy to deny playing with.

SUPPLIES

- four 11" wooden letters
- four 12" x 12" pieces of patterned paper
- acrylic paint
- five 4" x 3" pieces of chipboard
- five 4" x 3" photos
- two patterned paper tags
- bookplate and bulldog clip
- two screws
- two 12" lengths of ribbon
- cardstock

TOOLS

- foam brushes
- brayer
- craft knife
- self-healing cutting mat
- sanding block
- emery board
- screwdriver

ADHESIVE

- Xyron machine
- decoupage adhesive
- dots

MATERIALS

12" wooden letters (Carolee's Creations) • patterned paper, tags (BasicGrey) • ribbon (Offray, Bazzill Basics Paper) • acrylic paint (Making Memories) • bookplate (Magic Scraps) • Annual Wide Normal and Annual Normal fonts

With plenty of giggles, wide smiles and spontaneous squeals of jubilation. . . we PLAY.

oversized wooden letters step-by-step

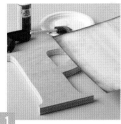

STEP ONE

Apply even coat of decoupage adhesive to face of wooden letter, using foam brush. Adhere full piece of patterned paper to letter. Roll brayer over surface to smooth out any air bubbles. Let dry 5 min. Repeat for each letter.

STEP TWO

Place letter, paper side down, on mat. Use craft knife to cut around letter, trimming excess paper.

STEP THREE

Smooth all edges with sanding block and emery board.

STEP FOUR

Brush acrylic paint around edges of letters and let dry 10-15 min. *Note: Don't worry if you get a little paint on the patterned paper. You can sand it off or leave it for a shabby chic appeal.*

STEP FIVE

Adhere all photos to chipboard pieces. Sand edges of photos for a weathered look. *Note: The chipboard will reinforce the photos so the edges don't curl.*

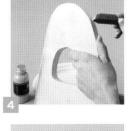

STEP SIX

For the letter "P," thread one ribbon through bulldog clip, wrap around letter, and tie in knot. Print text on tag (see "Printing on Tags" on p. 220), and clip together with photo.

STEP SEVEN

For the letter "L," adhere two photos to letter using adhesive dots.

STEP EIGHT

For the letter "A," wrap ribbon around letter and tie in bow. Adhere photo. Print title on cardstock and adhere behind bookplate. Attach to letter using screws.

STEP NINE

For the letter "Y," print text on second tag. Attach tag, then overlap photo.

Happy, energetic, curious, contented, playful and daring ...all encapsulated in one tiny body. You live every moment at play and are the most absolutely irresistible little boy to deny playing with.

one year later

FABRIC-COVERED CANVAS

I often pick up a home decor magazine while in line at the grocery store, and I always manage to find something that inspires me. Art canvases were all over one particular issue, so I grabbed two pieces on my next trip to Michaels. I painted the first one, but quickly realized that I'm not an artist. So I went fabric shopping. I brought home this rich, red fabric and the rest is history. (And check out the photo frame. It's a range trim ring.)

SUPPLIES

- 16" x 20" art canvas
- 20" x 24" upholstery fabric
- 8" range trim ring
- two 12" x 12" pieces of patterned paper
- 36" length of ribbon
- two 6" x 3" walnut inked tags
- 2½" x 5" tag
- bookplate and two mini-brads
- cardstock
- metal charm and vintage key
- pocket watch and watch face
- two 6" lengths of ribbon (⅛" and ½" widths)
- decorative brad
- stamp pad

TOOLS

- staple gun
- sanding block
- hand drill and smallest bit
- paper piercer

ADHESIVE

- photo tabs
- strips and dots
- clear, pop-up dots

MATERIALS

patterned paper (Daisy D's Paper Company) • bookplate (Magic Scraps) • dog tag (Chronicle Books) • mini-brads, decorative brad (Making Memories) • aged tags (7gypsies) • stamp pad (Ranger Industries) • ribbon (Offray) • vintage key, vintage pocket watch (*eBay.com*) • Times font

It is amazing to witness how much each of you change, yet remain very much the same.

Cole happily follows anywhere his 2 sisters lead him...and is often the inspiration for various games of chase.

Siblings by chance...friends by choice.

Just one year later it is amazing how much you have all grown.

In comparing these 2 photos it is obvious as to who is the sibling in charge.

"Coley, can Payton have kisses?" this is followed by a big wet open-mouthed kiss from her brother and is immediately followed by an, "Awww, he loves me."

fabric-covered canvas step-by-step

STEP ONE
Stretch fabric around canvas, and attach in back with staple gun.

STEP TWO
Overlap patterned papers and adhere to fabric with photo tabs.

STEP THREE
Trim 8" x 10" photo to fit behind ring. Adhere photo to ring at top and bottom only, using dots.

STEP FOUR
Position photo ring on fabric background. Tie ring to canvas by threading ribbon through left side of ring, wrapping both ends around back of board, and threading back through right side of ring. Tie ribbon in knot.

STEP FIVE
Use dots to adhere tags and photo down right side of canvas. *Note: For an aged look, gently rub the stamp pad across the edges of the tags before adhering to the canvas.*

STEP SIX
Print text on cardstock and cut into strips. Adhere on top of tags.

STEP SEVEN
Adhere title behind bookplate. Attach to canvas by piercing holes through tag, then securing bookplate with mini-brads.

STEP EIGHT
To attach pocket watch to canvas, remove watch face and drill two holes in back of pocket watch. *Note: I purchased an inexpensive pocket watch that didn't work.* Use pencil to mark guide holes on canvas. Use paper piercer to create holes in canvas. Thread 1/8" ribbon through holes in watch and force ribbon ends through to back of canvas, using paper piercer. Tie watch in place.

STEP NINE
Tie charm to key with 1/2" ribbon. Adhere key to tag, using adhesive strip.

STEP TEN
Add decorative brad to paper corner and roll up edge of paper.

Helpful Tip
Creative Editor Wendy Smedley found the range trim ring at a consignment store, but new rings are readily available at large retail and home improvement chains. Purchase different-sized rings and arrange them on a wall as you would picture frames.

genuine

CLIPBOARD PHOTO FRAME

Go to your nearest dollar store and purchase the ugliest 8" x 10" photo frame you can find. Watch the expression on the cashier's face as you place it on the counter with a smile. When you get home, pull the glass out of the frame. Place it on top of an altered clipboard, add some photos and a pretty ribbon, and hang your new photo frame on your wall. Bet you'd like to see the cashier's face now, huh?

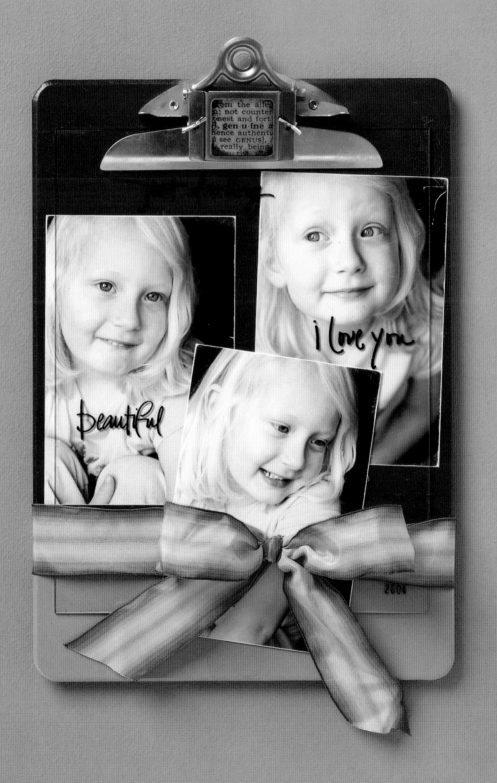

SUPPLIES

- clipboard
- spray paint in two colors
- painter's tape
- 8" x 10" piece of glass
- 36" length of ribbon
- rub-on words
- rub-on date
- transparency bookplate
- 1½" x 1½" cardstock square
- 2½" elastic with metal stops

TOOLS

- hand clamp
- sanding block

ADHESIVE

- photo tabs

MATERIALS

ribbon (Offray) • bookplate (Creative Imaginations) • elastic (7gypsies) • rub-ons (C-Thru Ruler Company, Autumn Leaves)

clipboard photo frame step-by-step

STEP ONE

Cover clipboard clip with painter's tape. Hold clip open, using hand clamp, and spray entire front in one color. Let dry approx. 24 hrs. Adhere tape 3" from bottom of board. Spray bottom with second color. Let dry.

STEP TWO

Adhere cardstock behind transparency bookplate. Attach to clipboard with elastic by threading elastic through bookplate hole, then wrapping other end behind clip and up through other side of bookplate.

STEP THREE

Adhere two photos on clipboard and place glass on top, under clip. *Note: I sanded the edges of my photos for a more weathered look.*

STEP FOUR

Adhere third photo on top of glass. Add rub-on words and date to glass.

STEP FIVE

Wrap ribbon around clipboard where two colors meet, and tie bow.

Project Variations

Not only is this project easy to make, but there are lots of creative options. Try these:

- Cover clipboard with patterned paper, using decoupage adhesive.
- Choose from a variety of clipboard sizes, styles, and colors. Mix small and large clipboards and create a wall collage.
- Purchase an easelback at a frame or craft store and attach it to the back of the clipboard, turning the clipboard into a tabletop frame.
- Make a clipboard for a teacher using class photos and memorabilia.
- Make a clipboard for a special coach using team photos and a thank-you note signed by all the players.
- Decorate the glass with foam stamps and paint, or a solvent-based stamp pad such as StazOn by Tsukineko.

Helpful Tip

You don't have to pull the piece of glass from a frame. You can buy replacement glass from frame shops or craft stores such as Michaels.

time

ALTERED CLOCK

Do you know how easy it is to make a clock? I certainly didn't when I first conceived of this project. I purchased a wood board and quartz movement kit from my local craft store, borrowed a few drill bits from my neighbor's collection, and whipped out my husband's power drill. Within an hour, I had made a clock adorned with pictures of my kids. You can make a clock out of almost anything you can drill. My creative wheels are turning already.

SUPPLIES

- 14" x 11½" wood board with beveled edge
- patterned tissue paper
- acrylic paint and water
- clock movement kit for ¾" thick surfaces
- 6½" x 9½" piece of cardstock
- 6" x 9½" piece of patterned paper
- stencil number
- clear sticker quote
- 52" length of ribbon
- decorative plate stand

TOOLS

- power drill
- two foam brushes
- sanding block

ADHESIVE

- decoupage adhesive
- Xyron machine
- 8" length of masking or painter's tape
- photo tabs

MATERIALS

wooden plaque, clock movement kit, clock hands (Walnut Hollow) • patterned paper (Chatterbox) • patterned tissue (7gypsies) • ribbon (Li'l Davis Designs) • sticker quote (Cloud 9 Design) • acrylic paint, stencil number (Making Memories)

THE BEST
INHERITANCE A
parent
CAN GIVE HIS
children
IS A FEW MINUTES

altered clock step-by-step

STEP ONE
Tear strips of printed tissue paper into 1½"-wide strips. Apply a coat of decoupage adhesive, completely covering the beveled edge, and press tissue to board. *Note: Be messy and overlap the tissue.* Let dry.

STEP TWO
Rub sanding block over edges to smooth and sand away excess tissue paper. Brush away dust.

STEP THREE
Whitewash tissue edges, using a dime-sized amount of white paint mixed with 2 tsp. of water. Lightly brush whitewash over tissue. Let dry 30-45 min.

STEP FOUR
With board horizontal, adhere cardstock to left side, and patterned paper to right.

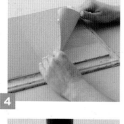

STEP FIVE
Use dial hands to mark placement for clock movement. Drill hole through board that's slightly larger than shaft of clock movement. Attach movement behind board following manufacturer's instructions. Secure movement to board with painter's tape.

STEP SIX
Paint stencil number and adhere to patterned paper. *Note: The "3", placed in proper clock face position, also refers to my children.*

STEP SEVEN
Add sticker quote to patterned paper.

STEP EIGHT
Sand photo edges and adhere to cardstock.
Wrap ribbon around board, over paper seam, and tie bow. Display on plate stand.

Helpful Tip
Clock movements come with hands; however, I chose to purchase a separate set of black hands.

nancy

TRAPEZE FRAMES

Hanging like an exhibit on a museum wall, this trapeze frame with its sleek silver lines is a perfect match for the hip Los Angeles lifestyle of my sister-in-law, Nancy. I filled the vertical frames with photos from her last visit, and the horizontal frames with descriptive words and thoughts of Nancy. With an eye-catching visual mix of text and transparency, the frames assume the color of any wall you hang them against.

ambitious, curious, sensitive, creative, bright

Nancy has always done things in her own free-spirited way, sometimes without caution, but always with passion, it is one of the things I admire most about her. She sees the world through youthful eyes, cares deeply for those she loves and embodies a confidence and sense of self that radiates from her.

ambitious, curious, sensitive, creative, bright

trapeze frames step-by-step

STEP ONE
Follow manufacturer's instructions for removing frames from trapeze bar.

STEP TWO
Center photos in top three frames, leaving ½" border. Adhere with photo tabs.

STEP THREE
Trim two transparencies to 5" x 7". Mark holes for screw clips and use hand punch to create holes. Place transparencies in two horizontal frames.

STEP FOUR
Print text on cardstock and trim to 4" x 6" (see "Printing Reverse Text" on p. 220). *Note: For an extra crisp look, print reverse text on photo paper.* Center and adhere with photo tabs in third horizontal frame.

STEP FIVE
Add rub-on words to glass, over photos.

STEP SIX
Reassemble frames and display on wall.

Project Variations

- Use the same frame to highlight members of your family or three different friends. Include text describing some of their qualities, traits, or achievements.

- Create a fabric photo mat from fabric that matches your home's decor. Trim your photos, leaving a ¾" to 1" border, then place the fabric behind the photos.

- Print your text on different colors of vellum. The vellum will give your frames a stained-glass look.

Helpful Tip

Umbra products are readily available at storefront and online retailers. Visit *Umbra.com* to locate one of their retail partners near you.

cupcakes anytime

MUFFIN TIN

In all honesty, I bought this muffin tin because when I walked by it in the dollar store I thought to myself, "Maybe not 12 muffins, but 12 photo frames?" I had never put much thought into decorating my kitchen with photos, but suddenly the idea of using a muffin tin to tell the visual story of my daughter's baking escapades made perfect sense.

SUPPLIES

- 12-cup muffin tin
- 7" x 10½" piece of cardstock
- 7" x 10½" pre-printed transparency
- 36" length of ribbon
- cardstock
- rub-on letters

TOOLS

- paper trimmer
- sanding block
- pen
- scissors
- 2½" and 3" circle punches

ADHESIVE

- Xyron machine
- clear, pop-up dots
- photo tabs

MATERIALS

transparency (Creative Imaginations) • circle punches (Marvy Uchida) • rub-on letters (Chatterbox, Chartpak) • ribbon (Textured Trios) • Times New Roman font

anytime is the right time for cupcakes

muffin tin step-by-step

STEP ONE

Remove any non-stick coating from muffin tin, using sanding block. *Note: The cardstock and rub-ons won't stick to the coating.*

STEP TWO

Adhere cardstock over half of tin, covering six cups. Trim and sand edges of cardstock to align with tin shape (see "Sanding'" on p. 221).

STEP THREE

Place tin upside down on back side of transparency. *Note: The transparency will extend to the edge of the frame.* Trace tin outline, then trim with scissors. Set transparency aside.

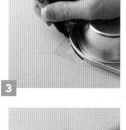

STEP FOUR

Punch three 3" photos and six 2½" photos. *Note: Turn the punch upside down and slide photo in the slot. Position the photo where you want by viewing it through the hole. Carefully turn the punch over, holding the photo in place, and firmly punch.*

STEP FIVE

Place transparency over cardstock, then adhere 3" photos over row of covered cups. Adhere transparency to cardstock by placing photo tabs on underside of transparency behind photos.

STEP SIX

Layer seven pop-up dots on top of each other and adhere to centers of uncovered cups. Place 2½" photos in cups.

STEP SEVEN

Apply rub-ons around cups. *Note: If rub-ons are not sticking, sand the tin some more.*

STEP EIGHT

Print title strip on cardstock and adhere to transparency (see "Printing Reverse Text" on p. 220).

STEP NINE

Tie ribbon around tin to conceal paper edge (see "Tying a Bow" on p. 222).

Project Variations

- Keep your eye out for the following items at consignment shops, antique stores, or estate sales and use them instead of a 12-cup muffin tin:
  - vintage pie pans
  - round cake pans
  - six- or 15-cup muffin tins
  - muffin-top pans, which have shallow cups perfect for photos

- Spray-paint your tin or pan to match the color of your kitchen decor.

love

PRINTER'S DRAWER

Hanging right above my desk, this vintage printer's drawer has been transformed into a dimensional scrapbook and is a haven for creative inspiration. Each small opening is filled with embellishments and tidbits of text. It's a personalized and innovative way to collage the things that matter most to me.

SUPPLIES

- printer's drawer or shadow box
- small assorted embellishments
- photos
- 40" length of ribbon
- silk flower
- brad
- definition stickers

TOOLS

- craft tweezers

ADHESIVE

- clear, pop-up dots
- strips
- dots
- foam squares

MATERIALS

printer's drawer, vintage keys (*eBay.com*) • assorted embellishments
(Li'l Davis Designs, KI Memories) • definition stickers (Making Memories) •
ribbon (Offray)

printer's drawer step-by-step

STEP ONE
Trim photos to fit over a group of drawer compartments. Place definition sticker along one edge of each photo.

STEP TWO
Adhere photos to compart-ment edges.

STEP THREE
Fill remaining compartments with small embellishments, using tweezers, if needed. *Note: I stacked clear, pop-up dots to secure and raise the embellishments.*

STEP FOUR
Wrap ribbon around the drawer and tie in knot.

STEP FIVE
Remove silk flower from stem. Remove center and replace with brad.

STEP SIX
Adhere silk flower over ribbon knot, using dots.

Helpful Tip

I used an actual drawer from an old printer's cabinet. Printers used this style of drawer to house small, wooden or metal blocks of type. I found my 16" x 16" drawer on *eBay.com*, but you can also find them at consignment or antique shops. If you can't find a printer's drawer, try using a collectible display box or a shadow box.

bright (brit) 1. shining with light 2. brilliant in color

christmas 2004

BERRY WREATH

The change in seasons often means a change in decor. This Christmas don't just hang a traditional wreath; hang a scrapbook. I made this one as a gift for my friend, Renee, from digital photos she took of her family. Use your own family pictures on a wreath to welcome your holiday guests.

SUPPLIES

- berry wreath
- five small metal frames
- four small photos
- small embellishments

- 48" length of ribbon
- cardstock

TOOLS

- paper trimmer

ADHESIVE

- Xyron machine
- photo tape
- dots

MATERIALS

berry wreath (Michaels) • metal frames (Making Memories) • epoxy words, frames (Li'l Davis Designs) • ribbon (Offray)

berry wreath step-by-step

STEP ONE

Wrap ribbon around wreath by weaving it through berry branches, making sure to leave 8" on each end. Tie in bow.

STEP TWO

Adhere photos and title behind frames. Apply adhesive to back of frame. *Note: I ran the actual frames and photos through my Xyron machine so that the surface area was completely covered with adhesive.*

STEP THREE

Arrange frames in place. Press each frame to berry branches and use strips of photo tape to secure branches to back of frame.

STEP FOUR

Use three adhesive dots to cover backs of embellishments, and adhere to berries. Press firmly in place.

Project Variations

- Add a little color to your metal frames by applying one to two coats of acrylic paint. Lightly sand edges of frames for a weathered look.

- Try using wood, leather, or canvas frames. Slide mounts also make great mini-frames and are available in a variety of sizes and colors.

- Add flowers and photos to a twig wreath, swag, or arbor.

- Create an advent wreath with pictures and favorite quotes. Mat a quote or small picture on one side of a small tag. Fold the tag in half and close it with a thin piece of ribbon. Assign each tag a date and open it accordingly.

- Create a wreath for each season. Each year add a new family photo to the wreath to document your own family's seasonal changes.

family of three

WOODEN BLOCKS

My neighbor, John, must think I'm crazy, yet he willingly offers his power tools whenever I ask him for a wood-related favor. This time as I carried the wooden rail post into his garage, he simply shook his head as he began to cut it into blocks. "They're not just blocks," I said. "Those are photo cubes." Randomly stacked on an end table in my living room, these cubes prove you're never too old to play with blocks.

SUPPLIES

- five 3¼"-square wooden blocks
- 30 pieces of coordinated patterned paper
- metal frames and photos
- bulldog clip, cup hooks, and screws
- rub-on words
- metal address number, word tag, and photo corners
- vintage key
- ribbon

TOOLS

- paper trimmer
- foam brush
- sanding block
- brayer
- hand drill or power drill

ADHESIVE

- decoupage adhesive
- dots

MATERIALS

patterned paper (7gypsies) • vintage key, photo corners, frames (Karen Foster Design) • metal frames (Making Memories, K&Company) • rub-ons, word tag (Making Memories) • hand drill (Fiskars)

wooden blocks step-by-step

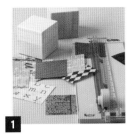

STEP ONE
Measure and trim patterned paper and some of the photos ⅛" larger on every side of block surface.

STEP TWO
Brush coat of decoupage adhesive on surface of block, and adhere photo or paper square. *Note: Use brayer to roll over block surface and smooth out any air bubbles.*

STEP THREE
Let dry 3-5 min. Use sanding block to remove excess paper edges.

STEP FOUR
Repeat Steps 2 and 3 for all block sides.

STEP FIVE
Adhere small photos, frames, and corners to blocks, using adhesive dots. Add rub-on words to frames.

STEP SIX
Mat photo with chipboard. Lightly sand edges. Attach bulldog clip with screw, using drill. Hang photo from clip.

STEP SEVEN
Attach metal address number with screws. Complete by adding miscellaneous embellishments to block sides.

Project Variations

- **Baby blocks**—Cover blocks in bright and bold colors. Babies also love black and white shapes and swirls. Stamp little feet and hands with a washable stamp pad, and decoupage the blocks with the images. Include important dates and information as well as memorable photos.

- **Kids blocks**—Make one block for each year of your child's life. Or, make one block for each letter of his or her name. Photocopy the fabric of a favorite blanket or outfit and decoupage a block or two using the paper. Include favorite photos and highlight the child's growth and personal achievements through the years.

- **Vacation blocks**—Decoupage blocks with copies of travel brochures, maps, or menus from your trip. Embellish blocks with coins, tokens, and ticket stubs.

- **Wedding blocks**—Create three blocks: one of the bride, one of the groom, and one of the couple. Include individual photos from childhood to the present. On the third block, include photos and journaling of the couple's courtship and engagement.

role play

CAROUSEL FRAME

I found this wooden carousel frame at my favorite consignment store for $7. Yes, $7. With a can of red spray paint in hand, I transformed the frame's brown, scratched, and lackluster finish into a vibrant red showcase for a family scrapbook.

SUPPLIES
- carousel frame
- spray paint
- cardstock

- rub-on phrases
- 4" x 6" photos

TOOLS
- paper trimmer

ADHESIVE
- none needed

MATERIALS

rub-ons (C-Thru Ruler Company) • Cezanne Regular and Sans Serif fonts

carousel frame step-by-step

STEP ONE
Remove glass panels and spray-paint carousel frame. Let dry approx. 24 hrs.

STEP TWO
Print journaling on cardstock and trim to 4" x 6". Insert cardstock and photos into frame.

STEP THREE
Apply rub-on phrases to frames.

STEP FOUR
Assemble frames onto stand. *Note: Facing text and photo should correspond.*

Helpful Tip
If you like the "spin action" of this project, but can't find a carousel frame, try making the Rolodex album on page 63.

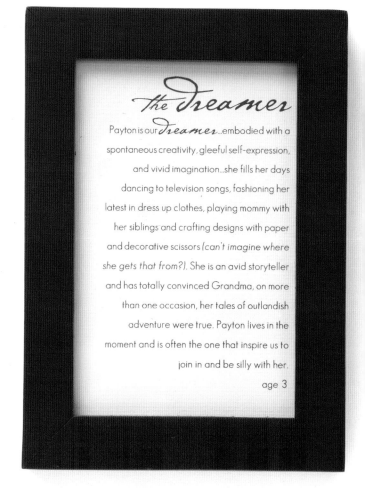

the dreamer

Payton is our *dreamer*...embodied with a spontaneous creativity, gleeful self-expression, and vivid imagination...she fills her days dancing to television songs, fashioning her latest in dress up clothes, playing mommy with her siblings and crafting designs with paper and decorative scissors (*can't imagine where she gets that from?*). She is an avid storyteller and has totally convinced Grandma, on more than one occasion, her tales of outlandish adventure were true. Payton lives in the moment and is often the one that inspire us to join in and be silly with her.

age 3

priceless

COIN FOLDER SCREEN

I love to reinvent something that's been around awhile. Take this coin folder, for instance. It's functional for collecting coins, but more enjoyable (for me) as a windowed screen. Dangle charms and embellishments from the coin holes. Highlight the panels with a few descriptive phrases, and watch your coin folder be transformed into an illuminating scrapbook.

SUPPLIES

- half-dollar coin folder (three panels)
- two 12" x 12" pieces of patterned paper
- 6" x 6" printed transparency
- paint chip
- assorted ribbon
- assorted charms, clips, stickers, and embellishments
- rub-on phrases
- four metal hinges
- eight mini-brads

TOOLS

- 1¼" circle punch
- paper trimmer
- pencil
- sanding block or emery board
- paper piercer
- hammer
- scissors

ADHESIVE

- Xyron machine
- dots

MATERIALS

coin folder (*eBay.com*) • patterned paper (7gypsies, KI Memories) • ribbon (Making Memories, Offray) • transparency, metal tag charms (K&Company) • metal-rimmed tag, "D" charm, spiral clips, rub-ons, hinges, paper flower (Making Memories) • clip, bottle, two-sided spiral clip (7gypsies) • woven label (me & my BIG ideas) • number sticker (Sticker Studio)

coin folder screen step-by-step

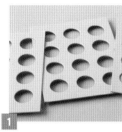

STEP ONE
Remove paper folder backing and detach the three coin panels from one another. *Note: I had to tear mine off.*

STEP TWO
Trace outline of each panel and coin holes on back side of patterned paper.

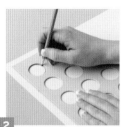

STEP THREE
Trim outside shape of panel from patterned paper. Use circle punch or scissors to cut out round windows around perimeter of paper, leaving the two center windows intact.

STEP FOUR
Adhere patterned paper to front side of panels. Use emery board or sanding block to sand edges for a weathered look (see "Sanding" on p. 221).

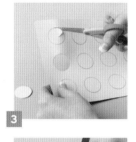

STEP FIVE
To re-attach panels, lay side-by-side, covered side down. Place adhesive dots between hinge and panel to hold hinge in place. Using paper piercer, pierce a guide hole for mini-brads. Insert brads from the front side of panel. Open brad prongs and lightly hammer flat to secure hinges.

STEP SIX
Place one photo randomly on front of each panel. Wrap ribbon around panels and through various coin holes (see photo on pp. 191 or 192).

STEP SEVEN
Cut transparency and paint chip to show through windows. Secure transparency to the back with dots.

STEP EIGHT
Embellish with rub-ons. Adhere stickers, dangle charms, and embellishments from open windows.

Helpful Tip
Coin folders are relatively inexpensive ($2.99–$3.50) and available at coin or hobby stores. Check online at *Amazon.com* or at coin collector websites.

Project Variation
Create a keepsake card, using a coin folder as the card base. Remove paper backing from coin holder. Trim or punch pictures to fit behind random coin holes. Use text and quotes to fill the other holes. Decorate with embellishments and ribbon. Mat panels with patterned paper or cardstock. Fold shut; wrap with a ribbon and name tag.

Make a birthday card for a friend or family member, using photos taken through the years. Include text and phrases that describe the person. Make a holiday card, using pictures of family members (and family pets).

payton

FRAMED CORKBOARD LEDGE

I found this adorable framed corkboard on clearance at Target for $2.24! I had to have it (plus the other two remaining on the shelf) not only because it was on sale, but because of its creative potential. Decorated with bright colors and simple embellishments, this ledge is a corky way to spotlight an individual you love.

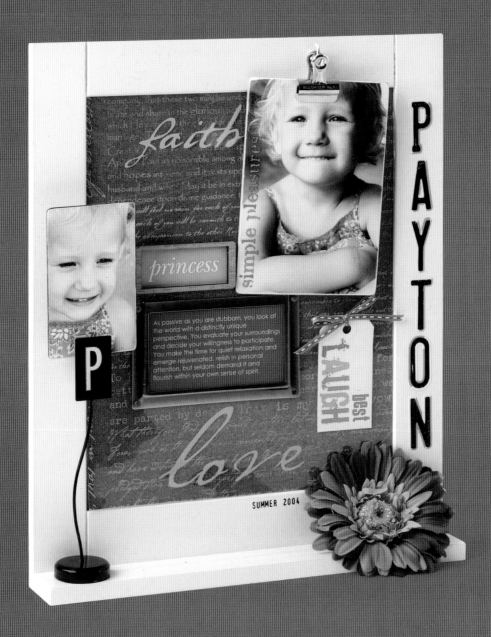

SUPPLIES

- framed corkboard with ledge
- cup hook and bulldog clip
- 4" x 6" and 2½" x 4" photos and pieces of chipboard
- cardstock
- two bookplates
- photo clip
- 2¼" x 3¼" tag
- 12" x 12" printed transparency
- 8" length of ribbon
- silk flower (bloom only)
- rub-on letters and date
- letter stickers
- mini-brads
- tin monogram letter

TOOLS

- paper trimmer
- paper piercer
- sanding block

ADHESIVE

- Xyron machine
- dots

MATERIALS

corkboard, photo clip (Target) • transparency (Creative Imaginations) • bookplates (Li'l Davis Designs) • brads, mailbox letters (Making Memories) • letter stickers (Sticker Studio) • rub-ons (Autumn Leaves, K&Company) • ribbon (Textured Trios) • tag (DMD, Inc.) • bulldog clip

framed corkboard ledge step-by-step

STEP ONE

Trim transparency to fit over corkboard and adhere with dots. *Note: Embellishments will cover adhesive.*

STEP TWO

Screw cup hook into top right of frame.

STEP THREE

Adhere photos to chipboard. For a weathered look, sand edges using sanding block (see "Sanding" on p. 221).

STEP FOUR

Print text on cardstock, trim to size, and place behind bookplates (see "Printing Reverse Text" on p. 220). Adhere bookplates to transparency using dots and brads. *Note: Use paper piercer to pierce holes through cardstock and transparency. Treat brads like push pins to secure bookplates to cork.*

STEP FIVE

Apply rub-ons to tag and tie with ribbon. Adhere to transparency.

STEP SIX

Place letter stickers down one side of frame and add rub-on date to bottom.

STEP SEVEN

Adhere flower to ledge, using dots. Embellish plain photo clip with tin monogram letter. Display 2½" x 4" photo in photo clip. Adhere clip to ledge, using dots.

STEP EIGHT

Embellish 4" x 6" photo with rub-ons, and hang from cup hook with bulldog clip.

a traveling home for artwork

PAPER MACHÉ PORTFOLIO

By the end of McKenna's first year of preschool, I had accumulated a mountain of papers. Of course I felt compelled to save it, and after weeding through the macaroni art and undecipherable scribbles, I kept all I could store in this portfolio. I covered the portfolio in bright colors to match McKenna's room. It sits on her shelf, and every so often we'll pull it down and McKenna will retell the stories behind her preschool masterpieces.

SUPPLIES

- 12½" x 13½" paper maché portfolio
- five 12" x 12" pieces of coordinated patterned paper
- 6" x 3" tag
- photo, trimmed to tag size
- brad
- acrylic paint
- ½" square hook and loop fastener

TOOLS

- paper trimmer
- brayer
- two foam brushes
- labeler
- craft knife
- self-healing cutting mat
- sanding block
- scissors or small punch

ADHESIVE

- decoupage adhesive
- adhesive remover

MATERIALS

paper maché portfolio (*stampington.com*) • labeler (Dymo) • patterned paper (KI Memories) • tag (DMD, Inc.) • acrylic paint, brad (Making Memories)

paper maché portfolio step-by-step

STEP ONE
Remove hook and loop fastener with adhesive remover. Measure left side of portfolio—front, back and flaps. Trim first patterned paper to size.

STEP TWO
Brush even coat of decoupage adhesive on portfolio and adhere paper pieces one at a time. Roll with brayer to smooth out any air bubbles. *Note: Allow all paper pieces to slightly overhang.* Let dry 5 min. Use sanding block to remove excess paper.

STEP THREE
Measure right side of portfolio —front, back and flap. Trim second patterned paper to size. Repeat Step 2.

STEP FOUR
Trim third patterned paper, and adhere over seams on front, back and flap.

STEP FIVE
Measure and trim strips of coordinating patterned papers for right and left sides, and bottom of portfolio. Repeat Step 2.

STEP SIX
To cover top section around handle, measure and trim coordinated patterned paper to size. Place, do not adhere, paper along top. At handle holes, mark hole placement by gently pressing thumbnail into paper. Use craft knife or small punch to cut holes in paper.

STEP SEVEN
Before adhering, cut straight line from edge of paper to hole. *Note: This will allow paper to wrap around handle.* Adhere pieces to top section, using decoupage adhesive. Measure and trim strip of third patterned paper. Adhere over seam.

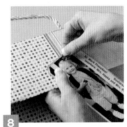

STEP EIGHT
Add photo and text to tag (see "Printing on Tags" p. 220). Brush acrylic paint along tag edges. Attach tag to front flap, using brad.

STEP NINE
Create strip of text, using labeler, to fit across top of flap (approx. 13").

STEP TEN
Apply thin coat of paint to flap edges, covering the exposed paper maché. Let dry. Replace hook and loop fastener on underside of flap.

love letters

PAINT CAN SCRAPBOOK

Some of my most prized possessions are notes, letters, and memorabilia from when my husband and I were dating. Yet, I'm embarrassed to admit they were tucked away in a rather tattered shoebox in the back of my closet. As I read through them, I remembered how truly important and integral these items are in telling our story as a couple. Realizing that they needed a more deserving home, I turned an ordinary paint can into a little time capsule scrapbook.

SUPPLIES

- 1-gallon paint can
- three 12" x 12" or 8½" x 11" pieces of patterned paper
- 3' length of ribbon
- 18" length of decorative cording
- four definition stickers
- eight washers

TOOLS

- 1" circle punch
- foam brush
- large circle template
- swivel knife and mat
- hand drill and largest bit
- pencil, ruler, and measuring tape

ADHESIVE

- decoupage adhesive
- dots

MATERIALS

Coluzzle nested circle template (Provo Craft) • ribbon, decorative cording (Offray) • washers, definition stickers (Making Memories) • hand drill (Fiskars)

paint can scrapbook step-by-step

STEP ONE

Remove handle from paint can. Trim two papers to 7½" x 11". Wrap, do not adhere, paper around one side of can and mark placement of handle attachment. Punch circle to accommodate attachment. Repeat with second piece of paper to cover other side of can.

STEP TWO

Before adhering, cut straight line from edge of paper to hole, which will allow paper to wrap around attachment. Coat each piece of paper with decoupage adhesive and adhere to can.

STEP THREE

Trace and cut circle from patterned paper, using circle template. *Note: The seventh circle from the center of the template is the exact size of the can lid.*

STEP FOUR

Adhere paper to can lid, and conceal any rough edges by adhering decorative cording along the circumference with dots.

STEP FIVE

Use measuring tape to mark placement of eight holes. Measure each set of two holes 1" apart and 4½" from the next set; drill holes. Place definition stickers between 4½" spaces.

STEP SIX

Thread ribbon through holes and around can, making sure to thread a washer over each hole.

Note: Drilled holes will have rough edges, so be careful. Gently guide the ribbon through the holes so the ribbon (and your fingers) won't snag on the rough edges.

STEP SEVEN

Replace paint can handles.

Helpful Tip

Simplify your project by wrapping ribbon around can instead of drilling holes.

Project Variations

Cover and embellish paint cans as:

- gift boxes
- storage containers
- trick-or-treat bags for Halloween
- cookie can for welcome-to-the-neighborhood gift

first year

WATCHMAKER'S TIN

I love anything with small compartments or drawers, so when I saw this tin, I flipped. As I looked it over at home, I realized that each of the 12 tins inside were like mini time capsules. Filling each round tin with an index print, small embellishments and a little text, I effortlessly transformed the tin into a dynamic visual record of my son Cole's first year of life.

watchmaker's tin step-by-step

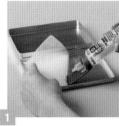

STEP ONE
Remove round tins. Remove any liners inside large tin, using adhesive remover.

STEP TWO
Set tin on patterned paper. Trace around bottom edge of tin. Trim paper and line tin bottom.

STEP THREE
Punch 12 circles (1¼" each) of patterned paper or cardstock; adhere each circle to one side of metal-rimmed tag.

STEP FOUR
Trim index print photos and adhere to tags, using pop-up dots for some. Add rub-ons, ribbons, charms, and assorted embellishments to tags.

STEP FIVE
Adhere tags to bottom of each tin. Add pop-up dots to backs of several tags to vary depth.

STEP SIX
Add rub-on numbers to each tin lid. Place lids on tins.

STEP SEVEN
Adhere photo to cover. Use sanding block to round edges and sand sides to fit shape of lid (see "Sanding" on p. 221).

STEP EIGHT
Print title and place it behind bookplate. Use paper piercer to punch guide holes for brads through lid. Place bookplate over cover photo and insert brads. Lightly hammer brad prongs flat on underside of lid.

STEP NINE
Print journaling on cardstock and trim to fit across two-thirds of inside tin lid. Add patterned paper to remaining third and tie ribbon where two papers meet. Adhere epoxy word. Adhere assembled paper and journaling to inside of large tin.

STEP TEN
Place round tins inside.

myrtle beach

WOODEN BOX

We always spend the week before Memorial Day weekend at Myrtle Beach, S.C., with Grandma and Pop-pop. Inevitably I take hundreds of pictures before our vacation is done, and I end up with pretty much the same photos as I did the year before (only we're all one year older). To spice up the monotony of our vacation photos, I covered a plain wooden box with my favorites from the trip and filled it with the ticket stubs and mementos from our afternoon day trips. I compiled all the remaining photos in simple albums that I keep tucked inside, and I even included a small tin of beach sand as a keepsake.

SUPPLIES

- 8½" x 8¼" x 1¾" unfinished wood box
- acrylic paint
- 8" x 8¼" photo and several 4" x 6" photos
- rub-on letters
- mini-albums

TOOLS

- paper trimmer
- two foam brushes
- small screwdriver
- stapler
- craft knife
- scissors
- sanding block
- paper piercer

ADHESIVE

- Xyron machine
- decoupage adhesive

MATERIALS

wooden box (The Weathered Door) • mini- albums (Making Memories, K&Company) • rub-ons (Creative Imaginations)

wooden box step-by-step

STEP ONE
Lightly brush 1" border of acrylic paint around edges of box top. Paint entire inside of box. Let dry.

STEP TWO
Using screwdriver, remove box clasp and back hinges. Set aside. Trim photos to 1¾" wide. Trim as many photos as needed to fit around the entire perimeter of box.

STEP THREE
Adhere photos to closed box around front, sides, and back. *Note: Use staples to secure photo edges to outside corners.*

STEP FOUR
Insert craft knife into grove of lid opening and drag around box, cutting photos.

STEP FIVE
Replace original clasp and hinges. Use paper piercer to punch guide holes through photos for re-drilling screws.

STEP SIX
Position and adhere 8" x 8¼" photo to box top. Trim photo edges with scissors. Use sanding block to round edges and sand sides to fit shape of lid (see "Sanding" on p. 221).

STEP SEVEN
Add rub-ons directly to photo.

STEP EIGHT
Fill box with memorabilia, mini-albums, and souvenirs.

scenes from the beach

supplies

Here are a handful of basic items I used to make the projects in this book. Most of these supplies can be found at craft, scrapbook, or office supply stores. Each project lists the generic supplies under the "Supplies" section and the specific manufacturer or source under the "Materials" section. If you find something that works better than what I've listed, then by all means experiment and have fun. There's no such thing as mistakes—just be creative. *Note: Some items listed in the "Supplies" section are not repeated in the "Materials" section.*

Acrylic paint
A staple in craft stores, acrylic paint is a quick way to get saturated opaque color or lightly-brushed white-wash on paper, wood, transparencies, and more. Many manufacturers supply archival-quality, quick-drying acrylic paints just for paper.

Binder rings
Steel rings that pull open, traditionally used to hold papers together.

Bookbinding tape
Made of strong linen fabric, this tape has a gummed tape backing and is used to bind pages to covers or reinforce spines.

Bookplates
Small metal frames, available in a variety of shapes, styles and finishes.

Brads
Fasteners with metal prongs that spread behind paper to hold the brad in place.

Cardstock
Heavyweight, preferably acid-free paper for paper crafting.

Chipboard
Thin, durable cardboard used to create covers and project pages. Check with your local scrapbook stores. Most wholesale packs of paper use chipboard to prevent bending during shipping, and stores may be discarding it without realizing its potential. Visit *dickblick.com* or *vanguardcrafts.com* for more information.

Eyelets
Small fasteners inserted into punched holes. Eyelets add a finished look once set in place. Available in many shapes, sizes, and colors.

Jump rings
Split metal rings used to dangle embellishments.

Mini-frames
Small photo frames available in a variety of shapes, styles, and finishes—metal, leather, and fabric.

Patterned paper
Offered in an assortment of styles and colors, patterned paper can set the tone for an entire project. To make your patterned paper choices easier, try choosing from product lines that offer coordinated sets.

Pre-made journals

Pre-assembled books save time and are easy to re-cover if you don't like the color or motif.

Prong fasteners

Two-piece metal clips that bind sheets of paper together, and can be found at most office supply stores.

Ribbon

Available in craft, fabric, and scrapbook stores, ribbon is an easy way to add color and texture to a project.

Rub-ons

Letters, words, and images that transfer to almost any surface, including paper, wood, fabric, and glass.

Silk flowers

A fun, feminine accent in varying colors and sizes. Use brads or eyelets for creative centers, or ink the petals.

Tags

Metal-rimmed tags are available in a variety of shapes, sizes, styles, and colors, while shipping tags—usually rectangular—also work well.

Transparencies

Clear acetate sheets used for printing text and images, or stamping. Also available with pre-printed text and designs. Lay them over patterned paper, accents, and photos to allow the images beneath to show through.

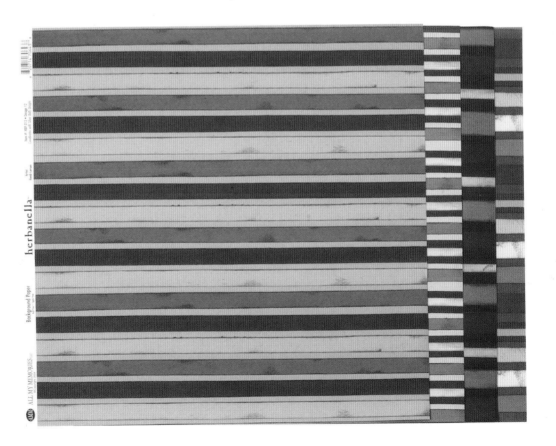

adhesive

All adhesives are not created equal, but that doesn't mean you can't make substitutions. Each project lists a preferred adhesive, but if you have something on hand that works just as well or that you like better, that's fine. Listed below are some of the most common adhesives.

CLEAR ADHESIVE DOTS AND STRIPS

Dots
Small circles of double-sided adhesive. Available in a variety of sizes and thicknesses. Perfect for adhering small embellishments, metal and leather, as well as unusually-shaped or heavy objects.

Strips
Thin strips of double-sided adhesive. Perfect for adhering long thin objects, such as ribbon, to a project. A good alternative to hot glue.

ADHESIVE TAPES

Tape runners (refillable)
Applies transparent, double-sided, acid-free adhesive tape. Available in permanent and repositionable types.

Tab dispensers (refillable)
Applies squares of double-sided, acid-free adhesive tabs.

Dot dispensers
Applies rows of acid-free adhesive dots. Available in permanent and repositionable types.

Photo tabs
Double-sided, peel-and-stick, acid-free adhesive squares.

Double-sided tape
Transparent tape (like Scotch brand) that can be cut to desired length.

Pop-up dots and foam tape
Three-dimensional, double-sided adhesive.

FULL-SURFACE ADHESIVE

Xyron machine
Functions as a "sticker maker," covering the entire surface of paper with adhesive.

Decoupage adhesive
Commonly referred to as Mod Podge, this water-based sealer, glue, and finish is used best when covering a large project area with paper. Available in glossy, matte, and acid-free varieties.

Dot adhesive sheets
Tiny adhesive dots that transfer from sheets of release paper when pressing items, such as die cuts, to the dots. The dots attach only where needed.

Glue stick
Inexpensive alternative for applying adhesive to a large surface area, but best suited for paper-to-paper applications.

REMOVERS

Adhesive eraser
Quickly rubs away any excess adhesive.

Adhesive remover
Commonly referred to as Un-du, this liquid adhesive remover easily lifts stickers, labels, and all kinds of adhesive from surfaces without harm. Liquid quickly evaporates, and items are restored to their original tackiness. Remover will not harm photos.

tools

These projects require few tools. But listed below are the ones that will certainly come in handy as you complete the projects.

Bone folder
Once made from bone, these plastic folders are used to score paper or cardstock and create professional-looking projects. To use, create a crease with the tip of the bone folder. Then, fold the paper on the crease and use the flat side of the folder to smooth out the fold completely.

Brayer
A roller that helps remove bubbles under paper to prevent paper from lifting in the future. For example, after applying a layer of decoupage adhesive and paper to a project, roll the brayer over the surface to smooth away any trapped air bubbles.

Computer
By no means a necessary tool, a computer with a word processing program (such as Microsoft Word) can help you generate text for journaling, or print on cardstock or embellishments. Handwritten text and journaling works just as well.

Craft knife
A pen-like cutting blade used to trim paper in tight or unusually-shaped areas (commonly referred to as an X-acto knife).

Craft hand drill
Hand-powered craft drill, especially useful when binding projects and albums. *Note: Be sure to use a safe drilling surface.* Don't apply too much pressure; all you need is light pressure and a fast drilling hand.

Cutting template
An acrylic template-based cutting system, such as the Coluzzle, requires the use of a swivel knife and foam cutting mat.

Die-cut machine

An easy-to-use tool for cutting shapes and letters. It's like a cookie cutter for paper crafting. You can purchase a portable machine for home use, or use a larger machine at your local scrapbook store.

Eyelet-setting tools

Eyelet-setting tools consist of four parts:

Mat or board—protects work surface from damage when using tools.

Small craft hammer—applies force to eyelet tools.

Anywhere hole punch—punches an eyelet-sized hole in your paper or project.

Eyelet setter—finishes and secures eyelet.

Foam brushes

Inexpensive and disposable craft brushes are great for applying paint and liquid adhesives to projects.

Labeler

A handheld, turn-and-click label strip embosser.

Paper trimmer

A straight-line paper cutter, sized to accommodate paper up to 12" wide, with an extending ruler arm for measuring. Interchangeable scoring blades for paper trimmers mark an impression in paper, making it easier to fold.

Paper piercer

A sharp-pointed tool used to poke guide holes in paper. You can substitute a sewing needle or push pin.

Push pad

A foam mat used to absorb the point of pierced applications. You can substitute the reverse side of a foam mouse pad.

Sanding block

Foam core sanding blocks provide more surface area to grip while sanding. However, any fine- to medium-grade sandpaper will do.

Self-healing cutting mat

Made of a unique material that won't dull your blades, a self-healing cutting mat protects your workspace and cutting tool. Look for the type with easy-to-read grid lines.

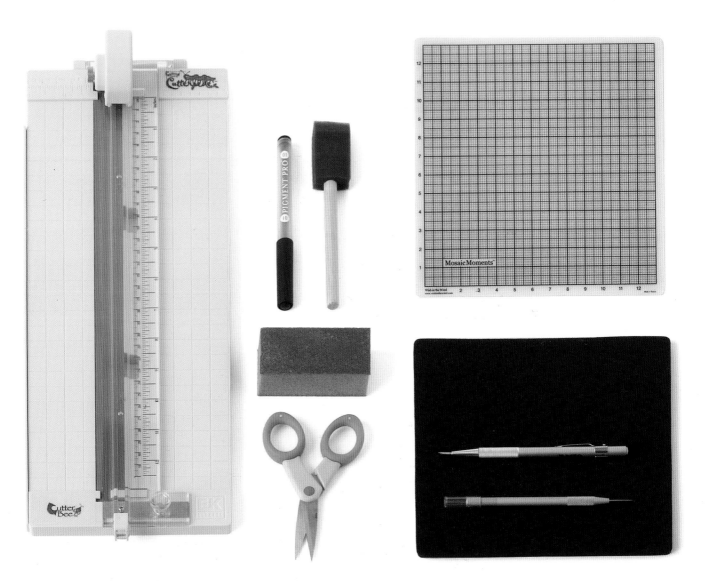

techniques

The projects in this book require only a handful of techniques, all of them relatively simple. I recommend reading through these techniques before you begin and referring back to them when you need help.

Wrapping Chipboard Covers

1. Trim paper, leaving 1" allowance on all edges.

2. Apply adhesive to back side of paper.

3. Center chipboard over back side of paper and adhere.

4. Fold over corners, then wrap excess paper around chipboard. *Note: Folding the corners first will create a nice seam. You can use the flat side of a bone folder to secure the folds.*

Assembling Accordion Pages

1. Cut 12" x 12" cardstock into strips. The width of the strips will depend on how tall you want your album—for example, 12" x 2", 12" x 4", or 12" x 6". The number of strips will determine how long you want your album.

2. Accordion-fold each strip, using a bone folder (see "Bone folder" on p. 215). The width of each fold will determine the width of the finished album. For example, fold every 2", 3", or 4".

3. Adhere the last panel of one strip under the first panel of the next strip.

Using Decoupage Adhesive

1. Wipe surface clean of any dust or dirt.

2. Adhere the paper to the surface by either brushing a smooth layer of decoupage adhesive directly onto the surface or onto the back of the paper. If the paper is thin, such as tissue paper, it's best to apply the adhesive directly to the surface. *Note: Use a clean foam brush to apply the adhesive.*

3. Lay paper in place, gently adjusting the position as you like. Firmly press in place.

4. Smooth with paper towel, making sure to wipe away any excess adhesive.

5. Starting at the center of the paper, roll a brayer over the surface to smooth away any trapped air bubbles or wrinkles. *Note: You can also use a bone folder to smooth the paper.*

6. Let dry completely. *Note: A decoupage adhesive made specifically for paper usually dries in 10 min.*

7. If you want to seal the paper, brush a coat of decoupage adhesive over the entire surface. Let dry and brush on a second coat.

Setting Eyelets

(See "Eyelet-setting tools" on p. 216)

1. Place pointed end of anywhere hole punch on spot where you want eyelet. Hit firmly with the hammer to create hole.

2. Lay eyelet upside down; place hole over eyelet.

3. Place setter into eyelet, and hammer firmly to set eyelet in place. *Note: The force of the hammer will cause the eyelet back to "flower" and secure to the page.*

4. Remove setter, and hammer eyelet once or twice to flatten completely. Turn over.

Inking

To achieve a weathered, vintage look, gently rub a stamp pad across the edges of your pages or project.

Chalking

For a more dramatic aged look, ink your cardstock, then immediately use a cotton ball to rub a small amount of grey chalk over your ink. As it is drying, the ink will absorb the chalk.

techniques

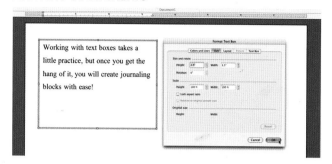

Printing Journaling

There are two ways to print journaling in Microsoft Word. (For both ways, make sure you measure the finished size of the journaling area.)

1. Set margins
   a. Open a new Word document.
   b. Make sure there is a visible ruler running across the top of your document. If not, click View > Ruler.
   c. To set margins, click File > Page Setup. Based on the finished size of your journaling, type in margin sizes for the top, bottom, left, and right. Click OK.
   d. The new margins will be represented by highlighted sections on the page rulers.

2. Create text box
   a. Follow Steps a and b above.
   b. Click Insert > Text Box. Click and drag mouse to draw text box.
   c. Click Format > Text Box > Size. Set the size of the text box the same as the finished size of your journaling area. Click OK. *Note: To remove box lines, click Format > Text Box > Colors and Lines. Select "No Fill" for Fill/Color. Select "No Line" for Line/Color.*
   d. Type journaling and print.

Printing Text on Tags

1. Type and print test page on copy paper.
2. Hold test page up to light and position tag behind text to ensure text will fit on tag.
3. Adhere tag over text using repositionable adhesive.
4. Reload test page and print text on tag. *Note: It's easier to print on tags (especially metal-rimmed tags) using a top-loading printer.* Remove tag and rub off adhesive.

Printing Reverse Text

1. Create a text box by clicking Insert > Text Box.
2. Change the background color by clicking Format > Text Box > Colors and Lines. Select the color you want under the "Fill" section.
3. Change the font color to white by clicking Format > Font > Font Color. If needed, center text in text box by clicking Format > Paragraph > Alignment > Center.
4. Print out on white paper or cardstock. Note: For crisper text, print on photo paper.

Sanding Paper and Photos

- To create a finished edge, sand the edges of paper or cardstock. Cardstock that is white on one side, or has a white core, works best with this technique.

- To fit a surface, trim the paper (or photo) as close to the edge as possible, then sand away the over-hanging edges.

- To create an aged, weathered look, rough up the edges of your photos with short, circular strokes of a sanding block. Try matting your photos with chipboard or cardstock before sanding.

Piercing Guide Holes

Add brads to your projects without bending or tearing the paper by following these steps:

1. Mark hole placement, using a pen or pencil.

2. Place paper or object over a push pad, piece of corkboard, or the reverse side of a mouse pad.

3. Make a hole with a paper piercer, sewing needle, or push pin, applying appropriate pressure depending on the thickness of the paper or object.

4. Slip brad through hole, or use a hammer to lightly tap brad through hole.

techniques

Tying a Bow

There are two ways to tie a basic shoelace bow, which is the type of bow most frequently used in this book. Remember, practice makes perfect, so don't expect to master this technique the first time.

Double-Loop Method

1. Cut a long piece of ribbon. If applicable, place the object you want to tie the bow to in the center of the ribbon. Bring both ends up to the top and tie a snug, simple overhand knot.

2. Form a loop out of one end of ribbon and hold it in your right hand.

3. Form a loop out of the other end and hold it in your left hand.

4. Tie a simple knot using the two loops.

5. Adjust loops so they are the same size.

6. Trim tail ends to desired length. Cut ends into a "V" or fishtail.

Single-Loop Method

1. Cut a long piece of ribbon. If applicable, place the object you want to tie the bow to in the center of the ribbon. Bring both ends up to the top and tie a snug, simple overhand knot.

2. Form a loop out of the left end of the ribbon, leaving a tail.

3. Loop the right end underneath the ribbon and back over the top again.

4. Form a loop from the right end and slip it through the folded-over part of the ribbon.

5. Adjust loops so they are the same size.

6. Trim tail ends to desired length. Cut ends into a "V" or fishtail.

resources

Listed below are some of the companies whose products I used throughout the book. Although some of these companies only offer products wholesale, their websites make for great browsing and often will direct you to a retailer carrying their product. Be sure to enter *www.* before each Web address.

7gypsies
7gypsies.com

American Crafts
americancrafts.com

American Kelco
americankelco.com

Autumn Leaves
autumnleaves.com

Basic Grey
basicgrey.com

Carolee's Creations
caroleescreations.com

Chartpak
chartpak.com

Chatterbox Inc.
chatterboxinc.com

Cloud 9 Design
cloud9design.biz

Creative Imaginations
cigift.com

Daisy D's Paper Company
daisydspaper.com

Diane's Daughters
dianesdaughters.com

DMD, Inc.
dmdind.com

Dymo
dymo.com

EK Success
eksuccess.com

Fiskars
fiskars.com

Junkitz
junkitz.com

Karen Foster Design
karenfosterdesign.com

K&Company
kandcompany.com

KI Memories
kimemories.com

Li'l Davis Designs
lildavisdesigns.com

Making Memories
makingmemories.com

Marvy Uchida
uchida.com

May Arts
mayarts.com

Mustard Moon
mustardmoon.com

My Mind's Eye
frame-ups.com

Offray
offray.com

Paper Addict
paperaddict.com

Paper House Productions
paperhouseproductions.com

Pebbles Inc.
pebblesinmypocket.com

Plaid
plaidonline.com

Provo Craft
provocraft.com

Ranger Industries
rangerink.com

SEI
shopsei.com

Scrapworks
scrapworks.com

Sizzix
sizzix.com

Stampington & Company
stampington.com

Sticker Studio
stickerstudio.com

Textured Trios
michaels.com

Two Peas in a Bucket
twopeasinabucket.com

Umbra
umbra.com

Xyron
xyron.com

RETAIL STORES

Scrapbooks 'N More
scrapbooksnmorenc.com

Michaels
michaels.com

Target
target.com

DOCUMENT

INSPIRE

PLAY

LIVE

CAROLYN VAUGHN PHOTOGRAPHY

A self-proclaimed "paper product junkie," Donna notes that scrapbooking was the ideal extension of her paper and photography addictions. As a contributing editor to *Simple Scrapbooks* magazine, she plays with the latest and greatest products, yet manages to keep the projects—and the process—simple and do-able.

Donna travels and teaches at scrapbook events across the country, inspiring students to think outside of the traditional scrapbook box while still preserving their memories in a meaningful way.

A former elementary school teacher, Donna is a stay-at-home mom to her three children, McKenna, Payton and Cole. Originally from the Jersey shore, she now lives in North Carolina, where she spends time with her family and teaches at her local scrapbook store. She tries to steal as much quiet time as she can to scrapbook. In her busy world, this usually means she kicks it into gear at 1 a.m.